# A FATHER'S CRY
# FOR MEANING

## SRI BURUGAPALLI

*Dedicated to every ordinary person*
*fighting their way forward*
*in this uncertain journey together.*

# Contents

# A FATHER'S CRY
# FOR MEANING

# PART I

## HAVING TO GROW UP FAST

*Lift yourself by your own free will*
*Do not be weak and lower yourself*
*Your free will is your only friend*
*Your free will is your only enemy.*

*– The Gita*

# 1

## My Own Personal Great Expectations

**A FATHER'S DREAM**
**FALL 2011**

ONE DAY, WHEN I WAS ABOUT 40, I returned early from a business trip wanting to surprise my wife and baby. I remember the scene quite vividly. It was a pleasant Friday afternoon in the fall, in Charlotte, North Carolina. My daughter was about seven months old, growing fast and was able to recognize faces. At the time I was the president of a multinational firm which required me to be away on frequent international trips, over 200 days each year, for weeks at a time. When I returned from my travels, I noticed that my daughter shied away from me and would cling to my wife. She was obviously unsure who I was given that I was appearing and disappearing all the time.

Each visit home it seemed that by the time she got used to me, I had to leave again. I tried to make up for my absence by talking with her over FaceTime, so she could see me and hear my voice. Often

Meena, my wife, would leave an iPad in the baby's room so no matter where I was, I could watch her playing. It was a strange situation. I felt like a kid obsessed with a new toy but never playing with it.

Although I would be thousands of miles away, my heart and mind were at home. I didn't like leaving them, unlike before we had a child, when I wouldn't think twice about jumping on an airplane even at the last minute and be away for weeks.

When I got home early that night, my daughter was crawling around the bedroom floor playing with her toys. Hearing my voice, she looked up at me with a confused expression for a few seconds. Then she excitedly crawled toward the iPad, looking at the screen and then at me, back and forth again and again. Her little brain was trying to process what or who I was. On my way home I had imagined she would immediately eagerly crawl towards me, smiling and jumping into my arms.

I was devastated. I felt extremely dejected, perhaps an exaggerated and odd reaction in some ways, but it affected me deeply. Although a completely innocent act, this episode, combined with her preference to be held by her mother, felt like rejection, and a personal failure for not being able to connect with my baby. Not being emotionally close to your child hurts, and in my case, it was strangely acute because I had longed for parental love and sibling relationships my whole life. I think children and parents thrive on the warmth of the bond between them.

That episode brought back memories of my own childhood and the pain it caused everyone involved. It must have been gut-wrenching for my mother to send me away, to comply with my father's wishes. I always wondered what it takes to make such a choice in the first place and the societal and environmental circumstances that make this choice necessary. I always imagined he must have passionately hated it.

I thought I would avoid the sort of situation my father found himself in, sacrificing his opportunity for a truly close relationship with me. I did not want to secure my own future at the expense of the bond between parent and child. His actions, while partially understandable, left me with unresolved questions if children who go through such separation ever overcome their unfulfilled need for family bonding. I know that in my case I didn't get over it and I was not going to repeat the trauma I and my family suffered because of it.

. . .

## SPRING 1975

My mother was named Prabhavati, and my father Prabhakar, both variations on a Sanskrit word meaning one who radiates light. It was as though right from the beginning they were meant to be together. They were first cousins by birth. My father's mother, Nanamma, was the sister of Rao Tatha[1] who was my mother's father and lived in a nearby village. In the Hindu tradition and particularly South India it is culturally accepted and common to marry within the larger family group. Marriage between "cross cousins" children born to a brother and sister, but not two sisters or two brothers, was not just acceptable, but encouraged.

I guess it's possible that it was seen as a good answer to the complicated situation surrounding arranged marriages. My father was Rao Tatha's favorite nephew. Nanamma was the heart and soul of my father's household, a tall lady with a light complexion and a regal stature, she was the oldest of nine siblings from a wealthy family, and was at that point the family's matriarch, respected by Rao Tatha and the whole extended family. It was her wish that my father be married to my mother. When my parents were the right age, their families set up their marriage in accordance with Nanamma's desire. My parents both duly complied with their parents' decision, and were married, after which my mother moved to our native village.

My mother told me the most difficult decision she ever made in her life was about me. It was when I was three and a half years old. For some context to this choice: my father had seen his friends and their children find success because they had a good education. With their academic credentials they were able to get excellent jobs or start and run successful businesses.

Despite how good our family's life had been for generations in our native village, he wanted me, the oldest and only son, to have

---

[1] *Tatha*, grandfather in Telugu

more. He believed this could be achieved by getting a good education. My mother did not have an extensive education even though her family had the means. Believing girls didn't need to study beyond a certain age, they sent her to a junior college close to their village. My father had studied at a private high school but dropped out in the tenth grade; he didn't have a high opinion of his own education.

Even though he lacked a formal education he was an ambitious man who did his best to run several businesses. He was naturally charming, gregarious, and very much a people person. He was a community leader in the village, and he often seemed to be the center of attention with a magnetic personality, his boisterous laughter, and a no-nonsense attitude.

My family had lived in our village, Vundrajavaram, for innumerable generations. It is one of the more prosperous villages in the state of Andhra Pradesh in South India. The land the village occupied was some of the most valuable in the entire state and was sought after for agricultural production. It benefited from its location between major tributaries of the Godavari River, one of the largest rivers in the region. This created a very fertile belt in the coastal area.

The village had about 10,000 people, mostly poor farmers, day laborers, and about a hundred major landowners, a few of whom were wealthy by Indian standards. Due to the explosive growth in the Indian economy, they later became wealthy by American standards as well. It was an idyllic setting, with lush green fields, coconut groves, sugar cane, and banana plantations. The more successful landowners used advanced farming techniques with modern machines and tools. The proximity to another busy nearby town, Tanuku, made our village a thriving community. It was also one of the more developed villages with an electricity grid, telecom facilities, and paved roads.

At this time India's government was more socialist and had programs building and providing a wide range of public services and infrastructure. In our village the government had established two nationalized bank branches, and a big post office, as well as large elementary, middle, and high schools—still a rarity for those times. There was a community center used mostly by poor farmers for social gatherings, and a general hospital that provided free medical services for the community.

The village hosted weeklong annual harvest festival celebrations which were popular and well attended. There were also two large churches and a small mosque on the outskirts of the village in addition to several Hindu temples spread throughout. The main street that stretched out over a kilometer, was famous for its large bungalows and traditional Indian homes.

Coming from this village really qualifies me as a "country boy." Even though I was sent to the city for my education, the influence of growing up in that rural village environment had a lasting effect. I always felt at home there. The summer vacations I spent back in the village were some of the most wonderful times of my childhood. Even to this day I find myself drawn to greenery, pasture, and farmlands over other environments, especially urban.

Our household consisted of me, my father, my mother, my father's mother, Nanamma and my two younger sisters Deepa and Sasi. We shared the same family lineage as most of the neighbors, with several of them being close relatives: first, second, once removed and twice removed cousins. Our house was in the wealthier part of the village where landowners had their high walled three-storied gated estates.

While our ancestral home was large with a lot of land, the house we lived in wasn't as large or modern as many of the others on the street. Our house had electricity and three bedrooms, a kitchen, living and dining rooms, a large veranda, a generous courtyard with two privy's and two baths and a well for water. In contrast to that of our wealthy neighbors, our house did not have a refrigerator, TV, telephone, air conditioner, or any other modern appliances.

Having a large family was considered a sign of prosperity in rural India for a long time. One of the economic results of large families was the continued subdivision of landholdings among the heirs as it was inherited over the generations. As time passed, the productivity of the family's landholdings dwindled, but my father had managed to build our modest house. His total financial assets consisted of a portion of the adjacent home and his share of the family's agricultural lands and his small businesses.

Several local families flourished and became very successful over time. A few enterprising farming families whose landholdings were shrinking, started moving away from the village. They raised capital by selling their more valuable properties in the village and relocated in search of cheaper lands with better long-term prospects in areas that would develop in time.

My father was proud of his village and loved everything about it, despite its drawbacks and his reservations about raising me in that environment. He did not want to move away and instead chose to remain there. He was accustomed to improving his family's prospects. So, he invested in multiple small businesses, hoping to improve his fortunes.

Traditional village life is extremely insular and simultaneously charged. Living among the same families for generations means individual family possessions are valued dearly and protected fiercely. While our house did not have much, one thing that stands out as an odd family relic from better days, was a six-foot-high bank safe conspicuously occupying the living room, like a grand piano in an American home. It was so big that it took six men to slide it four feet. Although it held nothing important: a little cash, some of my mother's jewelry, and old legal documents, getting rid of it was not a possibility. The family's only other truly prized possession was my mother's, a wedding gift from her parents. She was given an intricately hand-carved rosewood bedroom set.

To give some sense of what the daily life was like for a socially-well placed but economically distressed family like mine when I was a child, I should point out that back then the local doctor made rounds of all the homes on the main street, including ours, in person before going to his office; the barber came to give my father a daily shave and weekly haircuts. We had a main servant who attended to the family's daily needs, my mother had two domestic helpers, and my father employed farm hands to work at the farm. Many women from homes with social standing did not venture out into the bazaars or streets for shopping. When my mother or Nanamma wanted to buy clothes, jewelry, or other personal items, the clothing store and the jeweler would send things to our home, and the tailor would visit personally to take measurements.

Although I do not believe my family to have been overtly racist or classist, per-se, they may perhaps be considered so given contemporary social norms. I noticed that, as was the custom in rural India, the servants, farm hands and people from lower down the social ladder came in the house through a back door and drank and ate with utensils specifically designated for their use only. In fact, many weren't allowed to enter any rooms in the house and were restricted to the courtyard or the veranda.

The few luxuries our family had, combined with land and our relative social status gave my family a sense of comparative economic and social position. But it still stood in stark contrast to many other families in the village. However, I realized over time that our real wealth came from deep cultural values and a significant and supportive social circle.

Unlike most of the people in the village who kept to themselves and were uncomfortable with outsiders, my father entertained a very cosmopolitan group of friends, professional associates, and government and city officials. My mother often had to prepare enough food and drink to serve an additional three or four people for dinner. It was common for out-of-town guests to stop by our home, and villagers to meet with my father.

With his exposure to this group of people and his concerns about the shrinking returns from land ownership, he felt a good education would be the ticket for a brighter future for me. Learning to speak English was an essential start in getting ahead, particularly in our post-colonial society. In that spirit and unlike other people in his situation, my father insisted that his children call him "Daddy," rather than *Nanna* in Telugu. In what I would later understand as a telling difference, my mother always preferred to be addressed as *Amma* in Telugu.

When I was three, my father briefly enrolled me in a local Telugu nursery school called *Badi*. Based on the teacher's feedback, he saw I would do better in a more demanding school for my elementary education. The village's public schools, where most children went, taught in Telugu not English. However, he wanted me at a school where the instruction was in English. At this point most English language schools were private. Even the best local missionary school was in Tanuku. He did not have a high opinion of the local options. Even though most village children were tutored in English, they weren't proficient.

The state capital, Hyderabad, a city of two million, 400 kilometers away had the best schools, including schools that had English language instruction. They had better teachers, facilities, and students. In fact, the city seemed to have it all: an airport, multiple train stations, big businesses, major industries, large government institutions, museums, and massive hospitals. City children, especially the ones at the elite schools, were being prepared for success from an early age, having the best that money could offer. Most importantly we had family there.

My father was the youngest in his family, and incredibly close to his second sister, Satya auntie, who was several years older. Nanamma had six children, but none had any education past high school despite her efforts. All my father's siblings were wealthy land-owning villagers. Only Satya auntie lived in the city, Hyderabad, with her husband, Krishna uncle, a senior veterinary doctor for the government.

My uncle was known for his disciplined approach to everything, and he was committed to education, and raised his then four college-aged children in the city. He had a very strong sense of right and wrong and could be judgmental. He was quick to find fault in others, but also quick to praise someone who impressed him, and he was not easy to impress.

Krishna uncle's relationship with his three sons and daughter was not especially warm or overtly emotional. I always felt it was rather odd, although I recognize and understand the patriarchal aspects of the society. Still, the lack of closeness in those relationships was quite stark. Although the two older boys were closer to each other growing up, they fell out later and didn't speak much, behaving as acquaintances rather than siblings.

The four of them were 12-18 years older than me, one was nice to me, two were cordial, and the oldest was the most difficult. But none of that mattered; it was expected that I would adjust and adapt. Even though growing up I did not have a deep emotional bond with them at the time, later in life we became very close, and they were extraordinarily helpful and supportive.

My uncle's relationship with Satya auntie, his wife, was good. He respected her and sought her input wherever possible. He was also a devoted son to his sickly mother.

The usual definition of family, at that time in rural India, went beyond the nuclear family. It included the grandparents, parents, siblings, as well as the extended family circle. Everyone was considered part of the family and felt their collective well-being to be an equally shared responsibility among the entire group. The different branches of the family that got along better with each other felt this sense of shared values even more.

When I was a little over three years old my father took Krishna uncle and Satya auntie aside during a visit to our home. He expressed his desire to get me out of the village and move me to the city. He convinced them to raise me in the city at their home so I could attend a better school, but he wasn't interested in moving the entire family. Although my father was 13 years younger than Krishna uncle, he had a close personal connection with him, and they both respected each other.

It was a big request, but Krishna uncle couldn't deny it given their relationship. He shared my father's belief that moving me to the city for school was the best alternative. My mother had no idea that he had these plans for me and my education. After my auntie and uncle left my father announced that he was sending me to the city for school, and I would live with Satya auntie's family because this would give me the best chance for success.

My mother and Nanamma were stunned and my mother cried uncontrollably. Nanamma tried to comfort her, but she understood the plan. She sided with my father and reminded her that he seriously considered the consequences before making this decision,

9

and that he was doing what was best for me and the family. It is the nature of patriarchal societies, the head of the household makes decisions, and everyone falls in line.

At the time my mother was in no mood to hear it. She was adamant; her three-year-old son was not going anywhere and definitely not hundreds of kilometers away. She refused to eat or drink anything, going on a hunger strike, unwilling to engage in any further discussions on the topic. (Hunger strikes had cultural currency at that time in Indian society, following the Gandhian philosophy of non-cooperation in a peaceful manner, underscored by personal sacrifice as an expression of one's unwillingness to go along with a particular situation.) After a few days, while my father kept trying to appease her without changing his position, she was willing to talk about it.

"I respect that you may have thought deeply when making such an important decision for our son. But he is my only son. My grief is boundless thinking that he will no longer be with me. I won't be able to raise him and be with him every day. There are so many children going to school in our community; why can't he study here?"

"I understand how you feel about this," he answered. "He is my only son, too. Please think about how difficult it is for me to part with that sweet little boy, he deserves better than what we can offer him. I don't want him ending up like one of us here. I don't want him to have to stay in the village. I see him doing bigger things in his life which are only possible with a good education."

My mother was reluctant. No doubt, she wanted what was best for me. But the thought of parting from her child was eating her alive.

My father continued, "The sacrifice we are making will make a big difference in his future. I have great hope. Don't you want your son to get the best we can offer him? Why settle for less here? How many children will get this opportunity? Even the children of the wealthiest relatives and propertied villagers only go to the local convents. This is a special opportunity for him. My sister agreed to care for him. You know how kind she is. He will be in good hands with her husband. So please listen to me, agree with this."

My mother suggested that if this was so important, they should move to the city as a family. But my father said, "You do realize we can see him any time we want to, any time you miss him. It is not that far, only an overnight bus or train ride away." It turns out, this was not true. To have his plan go through with as little resistance as possible my father made up a white lie to pacify my mother.

When my uncle agreed to raise me in the city, he laid down strict rules for my life and studies. I would gain admission to a school of his choice and must maintain good grades. My father, mother, and other relatives could not visit me during the school year, so I could focus on school. Those were his rules, and they were meant to be strictly adhered to, or Krishna uncle would not accept the responsibility of watching over my education and general care.

My father was not one to go back on a decision once it was made. Consequently, throughout my childhood I would only visit my family once a year for four or five weeks during the summer break. My mother was unaware of my uncle's rules before I left, especially the one about not visiting, so, while still unhappy, she complied with my father's wishes.

A week later, my father took me to Hyderabad by train. I was initially excited to go to the big city, not knowing what my future would look like; I had no idea I would spend most of my life away from my nuclear family and only visiting them when life's schedule suited it. No amount of pushback expressing my displeasure at having to live in the city, away from my immediate family, was ever entertained. It just did not matter, and the larger purpose of pursuing my education was the most important thing.

The only intersection of cultural practices and my desires was when I had to go home for the required rites when my father committed suicide. Death looms large in a culture where most people profess a belief in multiple lifetimes and karma.

Separation from my family, whom I loved dearly, was part of the price I would pay for my family's hopes of a better future for me. My childhood changed dramatically in an instant. I could not fathom the reasoning and actions of my elders. I loved my mother and father and didn't understand what was really happening. Children are often unaware or usually do not understand the reasons and workings of the adult minds around them that direct their lives. I now realize the positions and difficulties of the adults in my life when I was a child.

.        .        .

## SINGULAR PURPOSE
## SUMMER 1975

Right from the beginning Krishna uncle had planned a very regimented schedule for my new life in the city, even though I was just a preschooler. One of his house rules for me was to call them Uncle rather than *Mava* and Auntie rather than *Atta* since he felt same as my father on the need for good English in general. He was strict in his child raising philosophy. I was to be his project. He told me this every chance he got, "Your singular goal in life is to make something out of yourself. Otherwise, why do I bother keeping you at my home in the city?"

The reality is that I was both lucky and unlucky to be his project. Krishna uncle was not a perfect man, but he was a good man. In many ways I ended up being his most successful experiment.

My uncle was almost 90 when he passed away in 2019. He was born in 1930 and came of age during the final days of India's struggle for independence. This had a significant impact on his views towards the creation of a new Indian society, dedication to government service, the recognition it brings, and its value to society at large. He believed in the role of responsible governance for social progress and the improvement of people's wellbeing in a newly independent country like India, and always stressed the importance of individual and social moral responsibilities and the value of education. Unlike my parents and grandparents, Krishna uncle's ancestors weren't landowners. His father was a respected bureaucrat in the British Raj and then in free India. He had raised my uncle to hold a job on the merits of a good education.

Krishna uncle had a reputation for being an honest public servant. A contractor once sent a box of candy during Diwali, the Hindu festival of lights, which auntie unwittingly accepted, thinking it a friendly holiday gesture. When Krishna uncle found out later, he hit the roof. Luckily it had not been opened. He returned the gift and scolded the contractor the next day for his ill-considered behavior. Everyone thought he was overreacting to such a small gift, but he would not take it. My uncle was proud of his rules and saw it as setting an example for others. He had an adamant, opinionated, emotional, quirky streak about him and his relatively controversial political and social philosophy generally resulted in lively debates. The daily news articles about banking and business scandals, high level political corruption and the like, he strongly believed that not many businessmen were trustworthy. He said that only crooks and cheaters made money, and those in business were only out for themselves. He had similar views towards politicians and people in positions of political power. He selectively associated with those he agreed with, and who wouldn't irritate his sensibilities and kept others at a distance. He was frugal to the point of monomania and was extremely averse to debt. His personal ideals and behavior taught me about right and wrong and the impact of his truthfulness, ethics, honesty, and straightforward approach to life still impresses me.

Really, uncle's only vice was smoking. He got into the habit of smoking cigarettes when he was in college and was a daily smoker until 55.

Satya auntie's role in the family was mostly domestic. She had a part-time maid to help her clean the dishes and other small tasks around the apartment. She kept a meticulously clean home and made special dishes for *Diwali*, the festival of lights and *Ganesh puja* a Hindu festival celebrating Lord Ganesh, the elephant God, as well as for *Sankranti*, the traditional harvest festival celebrated in South India. She cared for me, quietly giving me extra helpings, even though the food budget was tight because of the number of mouths dependent on my uncle's meager salary. Because of her love for her brother, my father, I held a special place in her heart. She always tried her best to be a surrogate mother, taking good care of me, staying up with me all night whenever I fell ill. Unfortunately, she was bedridden and passed away in 2023 due to illness, after my uncle passed away in 2019. Her oldest son, Karthi Bava[2], who I despised as a child, was a blessing to both my uncle and auntie during their old age. Unwilling to move them into a senior care center or a nursing home, he took them into his own home and limited his out-of-town travel for years, being home bound for the most part, attending to his parents' needs, with the assistance of domestic help, but still sacrificing a great deal. Auntie was rather proud of her own family, her parents and her siblings and raised her children to value family. She was not educated beyond middle school. She never asked for much, but I overheard her dissatisfaction on one or two occasions, with uncle for not being able to earn enough income to meet the financial needs of the family, she said they had to live hand to mouth. Her childhood was very different, having grown up in a large home with sufficient wealth.

After a few weeks of living in the city, Krishna uncle selected a good school for my early education. It was a co-ed school that taught in English in a convent run by missionary nuns. Importantly it was within walking distance of home. He felt it was the right school to ensure admission later into more exclusive middle and high schools. He was able to get a letter of introduction from a local city councilman, because apparently without this the school wouldn't even consider admission. The school also required an interview process. Compared to his children I was a real country boy.

Just like my father, I was proud of my village and everything it represented. Even as a child, I knew the special place I had in the hearts of many of the villagers due to their regard for my family, and so I had an unpleasant arrogance about me, not quite unruly, but boisterous, outgoing, and headstrong. Before the interview Krishna uncle made sure I knew basic etiquette and polite manners, and thanks to this sort of instruction, I learned to be more reserved over time, and smoothed out the rough edges of my rural origins.

Satya auntie dressed me in what she thought a suitable outfit for a school interview: a white collared shirt, blue shorts, black shoes, and white socks. The school was in a huge rectangular building, four stories high with three sides dedicated to the school and the nuns'

---

[2] *Bava*, means cousin in Telugu

residences on the fourth side. There was a large playground in the courtyard, with a stage on one side.

After a quick tour of the school, we were escorted to the Mother Superior's office. Sister Teresa, the Mother Superior, was known for being a strict manager. After greeting us and offering a seat across from her desk, she asked me a few questions in Telugu, and then in English, while reviewing documents from my uncle. After I answered all her questions she stood up and announced the interview was over. But I couldn't constrain myself, "Did I get admitted?" I asked, in Telugu, as we got up from the chairs. My uncle tried frantically to get me to be quiet.

Sister Teresa turned to me and replied gently, "We just finished your interview. We will inform your uncle soon once a decision is made."

I was confused and blurted out, "I interviewed you too. Uncle said you are strict. But I am not afraid of you. I like you. I like the school. Can I study here?"

Before she could even respond, Krishna uncle apologized and whisked me out, unsure about the subtle smile on her face. Sister Teresa later told him that if not for my speaking up, I would not have been accepted to the school, there were simply too many applicants, and many with special referrals from important people.

My uncle loved to retell the story for many years. "This boy secured his admission entirely on his own and at his age!" he would say proudly. Over the next eight years of nursery and elementary school, I became well-known to the teachers and especially to Sister Teresa. My grades placed me at the top of the class, and I was consistently nominated for head of the class.

When I first started staying with my uncle's family, we moved every year from one rental house to another, each near his office, in Vijay Nagar Colony, a very convenient commuter town. It had easy access to the Nampally railway station, and excellent local bus service. I don't know why we moved between so many homes so often.

However, five years after I had been living there, we found a permanent place in the same neighborhood. It was a 1000 square foot apartment with two bedrooms and one bathroom, on the ground floor of a three-story building. Our building was in a neighborhood with other large apartment buildings. Our apartment wasn't large, but we had a small backyard that was fenced-in with pomegranate and guava trees with flower beds, which we were quite proud of and showed off to visitors at every opportunity. I spent many happy hours in the shade of the guava trees, playing and reading books and giving away the fruit to the neighbors and friends. We remained there for the rest of my time in the city.

Krishna uncle was a stickler for his rules and discipline. He stressed that I learn to be punctual and responsible, and quickly corrected any deviations from his guidelines. He woke me at 5:30 am and took me on his morning walks. When I got home from school at 3 pm I had to complete my homework, including any additional work he might have assigned me, before going out and playing with the neighborhood children. And playing past 6 pm was absolutely prohibited. There was a large wall-mounted grandfather clock in the living room across from the front door, visible and audible from afar.

When it began to strike six, my friends scrambled to make sure I got home as fast as possible, racing through the alleys or jumping over fences across three or four backyards to get home in time. It was enough of a well-known routine in the neighborhood, that most of the children knew if I returned home late. Then my uncle gave me extra studying to do between 6 pm and 8 pm. Being late or getting homework wrong meant a thrashing either on the palm of the right hand or on my rear.

After dinner each night auntie put the folding cot out for me in the living room, wedged between the two chairs and a small sofa. Not going to bed promptly by 8:30 pm wasn't allowed.

My father had wanted to enroll me in every possible activity, but my uncle thought it was a waste of time for children to enroll in vocational training, sports, music, or drama lessons. He wouldn't even allow my father to buy me a bicycle saying it was unnecessary. My purpose for being in the city was education and not any other activities. Given my uncle's initial conditions to allow my stay at his home in the city, my father couldn't override any of his decisions.

My uncle wouldn't spend money on anything outside of the essential necessities for the home, but he took great pride in subscribing to two leading English and Telugu language newspapers. He encouraged me to read them, which I enjoyed, keeping me up to date on all the latest news. Newspaper reading was encouraged but novels or comics were not allowed. This led me to devour as many books as possible at the school library.

Studying hard and getting good reports was the only thing that really impressed my uncle. Nothing else mattered. His deep respect for hard work, education, mindful living, and good values and morals reverberates through my own actions 40 years later.

When I was a child, it could take two years to get a phone line into a house, cooking range and gas cylinders were rationed, even purchasing a motorcycle or a scooter had a one year waiting list. The Indian government set their economic goals around a five-year planning cycle that tried to establish production quotas. It was a loosely planned economic model rather than a western free market system.

During my childhood my family's living situation wasn't uncommon, when I first arrived at my uncle's home there was no TV, only a small transistor radio which my older cousins monopolized. I was only allowed to watch one movie a week on Saturday night, and sometimes sporting events, usually at a neighbor's.

Things stayed like this until about fifth grade when my uncle was promoted to a senior position in the Veterinary Biological Research Institute. With his new salary he purchased a black and white TV, which he later upgraded to color within a few months. And then pulling out all the stops he bought a refrigerator and a moped as well the same year. He still frowned on credit—if he couldn't pay in full, he wouldn't buy it.

Not having all the modern amenities enjoyed by my friends and relatives didn't really bother me. I think it taught me the importance of delayed gratification and living within one's means. Although amusingly we did like to say the fresh water stored in the clay pot in our house was better than the cold water from refrigerators, that is ... until we got our own refrigerator. For me, the biggest disappointment was not having a camera. I always wanted a picture of myself. Other than my class photo there were few opportunities for pictures. Those without a camera would either go to a studio or hire a photographer to come to the home. Photography was expensive and my uncle didn't see the need for such luxuries. The only picture I had of myself, until my eleventh-grade ID photo, was taken by an accommodating neighbor when I was in second grade. Upon noticing my neighbors taking some pictures with a small handheld camera, I curiously snuck up to the terrace and quietly watched them from a corner of the stairs. At some point my neighbors must have noticed me, as they signaled me to come over and then offered to take my picture as well, if I am interested. Needless to say, I was delighted and jumped onto a nearby table, quickly crossing my feet and sitting in pose for the perfect picture.

Auntie saved small change in a tiny box on the kitchen shelf. I was in the habit of taking one twenty-five paisa coin every morning on my way to school and stopping by the corner *Kirana* store. The *Kirana* store was a typical bodega selling basic household needs. My favorite Cadbury eclairs cost thirty-five paisa. But Agrawalji, the owner, always let me have the candy for twenty-five paisa. In fact, most mornings he was waiting with the eclairs and a big smile.

Sunday mornings, it was my job to go to the local butcher shop to buy chicken or mutton. That was the only day we ate meat because of the cost. Going to the *Kirana* store and the Ration shop to fetch things was added to my list of chores, which I was more than happy to shoulder. Each morning I would buy him a pack of cigarettes from the tin shack tobacco store at the street corner. One day around his 55th birthday, after a Rs 100 bet with me, he quit smoking entirely. This might have very well extended his life.

As a child living among the activity of the city: busy neighborhoods with chaotic traffic, street hawkers, corner vendors, and rickshaw operators, coupled with my uncle's budget-conscious home, helped teach me the necessary talents and skills to navigate the joys and trauma of everyday life and try to come out happy.

Sometimes my cousins bullied me, making me do their chores, kicking or hitting me, and making hurtful comments. I slowly acquired a thick skin for this treatment, but it sharpened my wit having to learn to respond to them. Standing up for myself became an important life skill for me. Thanks to this experience, to my surprise, I found myself capable of handling other difficult social situations: bullies in college, family politics, the workplace, and unpleasant clients.

"You are a tough boy," relatives and neighbors would tease me. "You are more mature than most kids your age." "You are a survivor." Hearing such comments gave me a sense of satisfaction as I thought of the difficulties that I endured at home dealing with a stern uncle and bullying cousins. "Just come live in my place for a few days, you will see why," I would think to myself.

On my birthdays my mother sent new clothes for school, but uncle did not allow birthday celebrations, thinking them frivolous, which always upset me. My mother asked once to visit on my birthday, but he became visibly upset and said "no," reminding her this was against their agreed rules and that my studies would be disturbed, and I would start feeling homesick after she left, consequently she never asked again. Occasionally my father was able to visit, but not stay overnight, he would go to a nearby hotel so not to disrupt the family's schedule.

While I was in the city, my younger sisters Deepa and Sasi were at the village public school at home. They enjoyed my mother's easy-going nature while my father and Nanamma showered them with care and love. Deepa is a shy and introverted person by nature, with a quick temper.

It is still a reality in India that a darker complexion is looked down upon. None of the elders thought twice about teasing her for her dark complexion. My mother tried to protect her the best she could, but the little girl was scarred to some extent from such comments. The social traditions have ended up splitting people into many shades of darkness and ranking them on a beauty scale, with lighter complexions getting the highest rating. Even as a child, Deepa felt left out, relegated to second-place status.

It seems this feeling has remained with her through her teen life and increased her insecurities. Years later I noticed her husband treating her like a queen, and for the first time, I saw her comfortable with herself.

In great contrast, as a child, Sasi, my younger sister was always considered to be beautiful, relatively lighter skin toned with sharper features. She was my father and Nanamma's favorite, of the two girls. In India nothing trumps a family's love towards a male child, and a single male child at that. So, in the social order, I always had secure status and a special place in the family. But Sasi had a near equal standing, boosting her innate confidence from the very beginning. She was talkative, smiling, and joyful person, and charmed everyone with her presence.

I wrote to my family regularly letting them know how I was doing and kept them up to date on my academic progress. I missed them and always asked that they visit. My mother never failed to write back, telling me to stay focused on my education.

My city home offered me the structure and imposed the discipline needed to excel at my studies, but I missed my family and village life. I lacked a certain sense of belonging. But my father had made it clear, that complaining about Krishna uncle's strictness or how much I missed my family in the village would not change his mind. He said my education was more important than socializing or emotionally bonding with my nuclear family. My regard for my father left me with no choice but to deal with the pain, but I think this helped me learn patience and perseverance. Whenever I missed my mother, I would wrap myself in the blanket she gave me when I first left for the city. During the last few weeks of school I was excited as I waited impatiently to get home as quickly as possible.

I developed the habit of saving money that anyone happened to give me, so that when I went home, I could bring gifts for my family. When I got home the first morning, I would visit my relatives and family friends, talking about school or life in the city, catching up with their families, and playing with the children my age.

On the hot summer afternoons, the children spent time at our farm. These are some of my most cherished memories. In the middle of the shady coconut grove, there was a pump shed for the well to water the fields. It had a tank to catch the water, and we used that as our swimming pool. We played for hours together, drinking fresh coconut water, chomping down tender cane sugar, cold watermelon, sweet toddy palm fruits and ice apples while trying to beat the heat.

I learned to ride a bicycle on those village streets. Imagine a chubby, short kid, with legs that barely reach the pedals, trying to ride Suraya the farm helper's bicycle, his most cherished possession. He would run behind me along those narrow village streets, worried about me crashing his beautiful bicycle into walls, canals, roosters, pigs, or cows.

One summer, together with some partners, my father set up the first and only movie theater in the village. He would have me make a list of my favorite movies for me to watch knowing that due to my uncle's strict rules I would not see them otherwise. Our theater routinely played one to two movies each week with multiple daily shows and would play most of the films on my list. All the neighborhood children would lobby me with their wish list, unable to muster the courage to approach him directly.

During the evenings, after dinner, my father would have me sit with him on our front porch while he read the newspaper and discussed current events with other villagers. Our porch was a gathering spot for the neighborhood. Poor villagers would frequently bring their problems and grievances to him for his advice and support. He would take on their causes and help with whatever was needed. He had their trust because of his judgment and a generous personality.

When an educated villager would visit, he proudly encouraged me to chat with them in English; I was happy to show off. My mother always baked my favorite Bundt cakes on a small stove-top oven, making sweet and savory delicacies and special homemade vanilla ice cream for me. I enjoyed helping my mother in the kitchen, churning fresh buttermilk during the mornings, melting ghee from the skimmed butter, preparing to make the delicacies and pickles on occasion during the hot afternoons.

One thing I was always strangely ashamed of was seeing my mother send the ice cream bowls to freeze at one of the neighbors' who had a refrigerator. Although it bothered her as much, she would do it for me. That was the only way to make ice cream. I simply felt diminished by having her do that and I urged her to get a refrigerator for our home and later promised to buy her one when I grew up. Given the amount of money my father spent on various other things with little regard to budgets, I could never fully understand why he wouldn't spend the money toward some of the household appliances that other relatives and neighbors already enjoyed.

At the end of the summer holidays, my father would take me back and drop me off at my uncle's home in the city. He would pay the fees for the next school year, buy new shoes, uniforms, books, all the other supplies before heading back to the village. He also left additional money for any incidental expenses throughout the year. He always appreciated auntie's taking care of me, and never wanted me to add to their financial stress. I was proud of this even as a child.

Anytime I overheard a relative comment on the generosity of my uncle and auntie in keeping me at their home, I would quickly chirp in with naïve pride: that I only stay at their home, but my father pays all my expenses. This was important to me, I felt strongly about not being a dependent and that my parents do everything strictly of their own accord, to facilitate my education, without any monetary help from anyone. I would say this when standing up to my cousins bullying me and teasing me about freeloading at their home.

The first month back in the city was always difficult for me. I hated it until I fell back into my routines, only to eagerly await the next summer break, longing for my mother and family. It left me with a deep void, always craving and wanting a family. It increased my love for my parents, grandparents, and my two sisters immensely. Perhaps being with them all the time, I would have taken them for granted or not loved them as much. I would have surely had some difficult memories with them like I had with my uncle. But only seeing them once during the year and having the good memories during those few weeks and then missing them day and night the entire school year, made me obsess over them.

The utter regard with which I held my father and immense love for my mother, the kind care for my sisters and pride in my Nanamma's wisdom and affection for me were all I would think of and crave for every moment. It is perhaps an unnatural expression of love, but it came from the separation I experienced.

At the end of sixth grade, it was time to apply for Middle School. The better schools only had a few openings because most students had been there since pre-school. There was a small number of open seats at the three best middle schools, and about five thousand students taking the admissions exam. It was a prestigious achievement to get in. My uncle hadn't enrolled me there for pre-school because the schools were too far away from our home, and I wasn't ready to travel on my own.

I placed first in three different school entrance exams, securing admission into those competitive schools. He picked the top-ranked boys-only school for me, happy that his efforts with my education were paying off.

When I was eleven, I could finally ride the public buses alone to my new school. But taking the densely packed city bus to school every morning was a circus. During rush hour, it was common to see over a hundred and fifty people packed into a bus meant for fifty, hanging on to anything. My skill in jumping off a moving bus allowed me to get on or off anywhere, secure a seat for myself, or save a seat by staring down anyone that may be heading toward it.

My new school was even larger than my previous one, with multiple playgrounds, huge halls, big classrooms, and recreational facilities. It was a good environment for students to thrive in; it was known for being academically rigorous and produced top students. For the rest of my student career there I had a friendly rivalry with a fellow student for first place. I was involved with the drama, debate, science, and biology clubs—anything the school offered for free.

Doing a school play I got a little carried away with my role as the evil villain, and I shaved my head clean and wore a dark headband; it made the entire auditorium roar with laughter. My education continued to go well, and things were seemingly going as planned, until my father came for an unannounced visit to the city.

# 2

## Learning About Endings

### A CHILD'S PROMISE
### NOVEMBER 1983

I REMEMBER THE FEELING I had when I saw my father's shoes outside our front door when I got home from school on a Saturday afternoon, it meant that he had come for an unannounced visit. I was elated he was here. I have distinct, almost episodic memories of my father: a sharp looking, medium built man with lightly curling hair and a neatly trimmed manly mustache, his dark sunglasses, the expensive imported cologne, the scent of Brylcream, his brand of cigarettes, his custom-made clothes, his wristwatch, and even his steel fountain pen.

With time memories of people can fade but those memories are deeply embedded as part of my own story of my father. As a child I adored no one more than him—my father was my hero. When I grew up, I wanted to be just like him: strong, well loved, respected, principled. I was completely overwhelmed at this unexpected, rare event, I ran into the living room with a huge smile and saw him having tea with Krishna uncle and Satya auntie. I rushed to hug him.

He looked down at me with a pleasant smile and tussled my hair, "How's your school? Do you like your new friends?" he asked while finishing his tea. I can still see him placing the empty cup on the blue deco-lam sheet coffee table.

I started to talk non-stop without even taking a breath, giving him every minute detail about my new school, my teachers, my friends, making sure I told him about my class rank. I remembered that I had my report card in my school bag, I ran to get it and Krishna uncle gestured for me to bring it to him. He reviewed it, asking a few questions. But impatiently I snatched the card from him and handed it to my father so he could see it. I softly pleaded with him, "Daddy, can you sign my report card this time? You've never signed any of my report cards. I want to show it to my teachers."

Smiling broadly, he pulled out the sleek pen from his pocket and signed his name in English.

He asked me, "Is there anything you need?"

I told him, "Yes, I need new shoes," pointing to the heel on my shoe that was falling off.

My father never really said much about his feelings, but I knew he loved me immensely and he never failed to get me anything I asked for. I was always reminded by my family how much his face lit up when he got to spend time with me, and I wanted very much to make him proud of me.

"He goes through three pairs of shoes each year and ten pairs of socks. I have never seen any child needing so many shoes," Satya auntie joked gently. He kept smiling.

After a few minutes Krishna uncle told me, "Either go out to play with your friends or go inside and study in the bedroom. We need to speak with your father in private."

I was not happy about leaving my father's side. But I knew what would happen if I didn't heed Krishna uncle's order. Normally I would go out, but not wanting to go too far from my father, I stayed inside. Leaving the adults to their conversation, I grabbed a schoolbook from the shelf and closed the living room door behind me. I sat at the table in the dining room, pretending to read, but really listening intently to the adults in the living room while peeking through a tiny gap between the door and its frame.

Their conversation went on for several hours, and the discussion was emotional, even heated at times. Sometimes their voices were just whispers, but other times it got louder, and Satya auntie began to weep. I could hear her pleading with my father to be rational.

I can still hear Krishna uncle, "Think about what you are saying. It doesn't make much sense. Don't be hasty. What will happen to your wife, the children? Who will care for them?"

What in the world could my father be saying to them? I was mystified. What do they mean "be rational?" My father always seemed to be a sensible man. He's the man that others went to for advice and assistance, not someone who I thought needed help. I always wanted to be bold, decisive, and helpful like my father. He was well loved by his family, his cousins, and his large network of friends. In his own way he was a fun guy to be around, laughing, joking, and ensuring that everyone else was comfortable. He always stood by uncle anytime he needed help, he even arranged for my uncle's son to marry the daughter of a close friend. I was proud of how people treated him with respect, but hearing Krishna uncle cautioning my father made no sense to me.

Through the door I could hear my father say, "I am here today to see my son, spend some time with him. I realize it is against your rules, but I had no choice. I hear what you are saying, and of course I will think about it." He tried to tell Satya auntie that everything would be fine. He started joking and laughing with them, it was such an awkward pivot that even as a child I could sense that something was wrong.

Later that evening, he left for his hotel and promised he would return in the morning and asked for permission for us to spend the day together and go around the city. I could hardly contain myself at the thought of spending the entire Sunday with him. It was all I could talk about for the rest of the evening. He had been to the city before, but he had never taken me anywhere. This would be the first time. But bits and pieces of the adults' conversation from earlier in the evening ran through my head as I fell asleep.

The following day, my father showed up bright and early for breakfast. He had hired a taxi for the whole day, and we headed out on our tour of the city. We visited his closest friends and relatives and had lunch at his favorite restaurant. He bought me the shoes I needed and more clothes.

At one point he turned to look at me and said, "I am pleased with how you are doing here. Remember always to study well and do your best. You will be the man of our house soon. You should always take care of your mother and sisters when you grow up," he pulled me close as we rode the taxi back to the apartment.

I looked him straight in the face answering, "I will study my hardest Daddy. And I will be good and take care of them."

I didn't understand why he was telling me this, but I was happy to hear him praise me. I had never heard compliments like that from him before. I hugged him even tighter. He told Krishna uncle and Satya auntie he would take the last train back home. But they urged him to stay, encouraging him to spend a few more days. Reluctantly, he agreed to stay just one more day because the next day was a public holiday.

I woke up at the first ray of sunlight, staring out the window and rushing to the door at every noise. He did not show up until around 2 pm, he looked haggard and tired. His eyes were bloodshot, as if he had been up most of the night. He spent the rest of the afternoon with us. After about an hour Krishna uncle asked me to leave the room like the day before, saying he had to speak with my father. I left but stood quietly outside, my ear pressed to the door.

Their conversation became intense, I could only make out pieces here and there. At one point, I could hear Krishna uncle making my father promise him not to do anything foolish, he agreed, promising he would think things over. He thanked them for taking care of me, but something felt off to me. The hushed tones over the last two days, and my father's earlier conversation with me, and now this other emotional discussion? I couldn't understand what was happening. But I felt uneasy.

Around 6 pm, he was ready to leave. Karthi Bava offered to drive him to the station. Satya auntie called me in to say goodbye, he hugged me and told me to take care of myself and pay attention to what Krishna uncle told me. Unwilling to let him go I said, "Daddy, I want to go with you and drop you off at the railway station," he quickly agreed before Krishna uncle could protest. It seemed that he didn't want to leave either and he would take any additional time with me that he could, and that made me feel special.

I wedged myself in between my father and Karthi Bava on the scooter. The train was ready to board when we reached the station. Karthi Bava took the luggage. I was clinging to my father the entire time; I didn't want him to let go of me. As he slowly settled into his seat by the window, he gave Karthi Bava some money to buy him a water bottle.

After he handed over the money, he put his hand on my shoulder and said, "You will remember what I told you yesterday about taking care of your mother and sisters, you will be a good boy and study hard, won't you?" Then pulling me to his lap as he stuffed a Rs100 bill in my pocket. His voice had changed somehow, his tone was different, his eyes were different, how he pulled me close was different. He was trembling and had a deeply sad expression on his face.

The situation felt off, and my heart sank. Before I could reply, Karthi Bava returned. The train was about to leave, and Karthi Bava hurried in telling me to follow him. I ignored him, holding on tightly to my father's hand. He walked me to the door and kissed me on the cheek as Karthi Bava had to yank me from the doorway. The train began to move. As my feet landed on the platform, I looked up to wave back; I saw tears in his eyes, he pulled out his white handkerchief to dry them.

I could hear my heart pounding in my ears, louder than the speeding train, louder than the commotion at the station, it was all I could feel or hear. My father had always managed to communicate a lot without necessarily saying a lot, and here too, he managed to communicate through the silence and the many unsaid words. Of course, I didn't know it was the last time I would see him.

The next day must be one of the most uneven of my whole life. It started out on a real high point but ended as low as it gets, the definition of trauma. The best part of school the next day was submitting the report card signed by my father to my teacher, making sure to point out his signature.

Then the flip occurred. It was 3 pm and I was in history class, when one of Krishna uncle's assistants, Sharif, came to the classroom door with the school secretary, they both had grim looks. They said I had to come with them, and I was being sent home for an emergency because my father was ill. When I arrived at the apartment Krishna uncle and Satya auntie were already packed and ready to go. As soon as she saw me, Auntie put her arms around me and started weeping.

I looked around at the bags and asked, "Did something happen to my father?"

She cried even louder. Krishna uncle kept wiping away his tears while asking her to calm down. They did not reply at first.

"Your father had an accident and is at the hospital. They asked to see you immediately, so we must go to the village right away," Krishna uncle finally said.

We rushed to the station for the first available train, and it was jam-packed. It was a nine-hour journey in a filthy, crowded third class car with standing room only for the whole trip. Indian rail journeys can require serious endurance. I was lost in thought; I didn't really believe that he had just had an accident. I was convinced it was fatal.

Most of the train ride I kept fighting back tears and wept quietly, turning my head away from Krishna uncle and Satya auntie, wiping my tears. When I felt a breath of cold air any time, I managed to bring my head near the windowsill letting the cool breeze dry my wet cheeks while I kept imagining the worst—that my father was dead.

A relative picked us up at the station nearest to our village which was about an hour away by car. It was 4 am when we arrived at the village. People had gathered around our house and as soon as we arrived, I was whisked quickly into the house. As I walked in, I saw my father's body laid out on a small rug in the middle of the floor: he was covered in a long white cloth. With the sheet pulled all the way up his body to his neck, only his swollen face was visible; his skin was darkened with a greenish brown hue. My mother was sitting next to him, there were several relatives and friends gathered around the room. My two sisters were huddled in the corner.

As soon as I entered the room erupted in deafening wails. My mother was inconsolable and held me tightly for as long as she could, drenching me in tears, her body burning up. Many older relatives, uncles, and aunts pulled me towards them, hugging me and crying. I had no tears or feelings at that moment, as though the wind swept away all my feelings along with the tears during the train journey and left me dried and emotionless. I think that having imagined the worst, that my father was dead, throughout the long train ride made me numb to the sight of his dead body when I finally saw him.

I was already disassociated from what was going on around me. I sat silently staring at my father's body for a long time, shifting my gaze from one person to the next. I was searching for my little sisters. I saw Deepa, ten, peeking from behind the kitchen door, Sasi, eight, was next to her, clinging to a relative's leg, staring at the floor, nervous to look toward the motionless body. Both girls were tired from not sleeping, watching all the adults sobbing for hours. The dark eyeliner under Deepa's eyes was smeared all over her cheeks. Sasi was half asleep, relieved to see me, wiping her tears. Seeing the three of us together made it harder for everyone, particularly my mother and Nanamma, as they sobbed heavily, and everyone wailed louder.

At sunrise, the body was taken in procession to our farm to be cremated, I was expected to perform the last rites. We went to the spot where generations of our family had been cremated. The ceremony lasted an hour. I went through the motions, doing everything the high priest directed, holding in my emotions, unable to fathom what was happening.

Every time the high priest chanted a *mantra*[3] invoking my father's and forefathers' spirits, a spasm of emotion coursed

---

[3] *Mantra*, a sacred utterance in Sanskrit

through my body and his smiling face flashed across my mind's eye. I desperately wanted to see my mother and be with her right then. But women weren't allowed to attend funerals in India. But I still wanted to run and be home with my mother, Nanamma, and sisters. After the ceremony, some villagers went to the mango tree in the middle of the farm. They didn't want me to follow and told me to remain at the cremation site.

"I worry how this family will survive now, who will take care of them?" I could overhear someone say as we walked back home.

"I wonder why he did this. He was such a well-respected man. This family will be lost now. The poor little children ... hmm," another said.

I knew right then why my father made me promise I would take care of my mother and sisters. "I know who will take care of our family," I thought. In my head I repeated, "I will not fail you, Daddy. I promise." But among several unpleasant ideas there was one thought that kept eating at me, "Why had my father done this?" As a twelve-year-old boy who spent most of his life away from his family, I hadn't spent an extended period with him, so I felt totally ill equipped to know what he would have been thinking. What had finally pushed him over the edge? I couldn't even really process the nature of my loss.

My father's death ended my childhood, and I became immediately aware of the real, final, and personal nature of death. I spent an immeasurable amount of time: hours, days, months, and years wondering how things might have been different had he not died and been around for me, my sisters, my mother, and the rest of the family. I even went so far to fixate on some of the smallest things leading up to the death.

What my life might have been like had he not visited, spending what was essentially his last day with me. I'm sure there is something about the fact that my father chose me to be the last person he really spoke to, but I can never get my head around what it meant. How much did I even mean to him, what had the family meant to him, and what did he expect me to do after he was no longer around?

.        .        .

## THE SEEMINGLY IMPOSSIBLE ACT
## NOVEMBER 1983

My father's funeral lasted eleven days. Each day, the priest performed a certain set of religious rituals invoking the ancestors' spirits, culminating in an elaborate ceremony on the final day where everyone gathered.

My father and mother had great relationships with their friends and family, accepting invitations, participating in events, always helping people. Even when friends traveling to our village had many relatives to visit, they still stopped in, stayed, and spent vacations with us. My father's death shocked everyone and prompted them to offer their respect and condolences to the family. More and more relatives and friends kept pouring in as the news spread.

On the second day, I overheard some of my cousins talking. Listening to them it became clear that he had committed suicide. I was devastated, my heart broke; and I could feel my anxiety rising, my whole body shivering. I did not understand it, and to some extent I still don't. I kept thinking to myself, "How could someone do that? Why would my father do that? My father! What was everyone talking about? Why do they stop talking or speak in hushed tones when they see me?"

I was now determined to find out the whole story. Over the next few days, I managed to piece it together, using every means possible to collect information, pretending to be asleep while eavesdropping on adults' conversations.

It took a few days, but I was able to put together what happened over his last few hours. The morning my father got back he was home around 7 am. My mother had been running a high fever for two days and had been sleeping in the main bedroom, but she was in no condition to get up. When my father came into the home, Nanamma was sitting by the edge of her bed on the veranda offering her morning prayers. She was happy to see him and told him about my mother's illness. She had been expecting him sooner and asked him why he was late. But he did not answer, rather, he walked by without saying a word. He paused for a moment outside the bedroom door but didn't go in. Setting his overnight bag in the corner, he went to the veranda and climbed up into the attic. He came down quickly, holding a round tin container. Shuffling past Nanamma, again ignoring her questions, he left the house with the container tucked under his arm.

My mother, being ill, did not hear what was happening outside her door. I always imagined that my father knew if he spoke to my mother, who he loved dearly, he would not be able to follow through with his plans. So, he avoided her, just as he avoided his own mother. He rushed to the farm with his dog, Jimmy, following him. To keep from being seen, he avoided well-traveled paths. He tried to send the dog home, but he would not leave my father's side.

When he reached the farm the morning work was done, and the farm hands had left. My father had made sure that he would be alone. He sat at the base of the large mango tree planted in the middle of the fields and quickly consumed the contents of the tin container. I can almost see his dog getting restless, being agitated, whimpering, and circling the tree, trying to jump on him. No one, except for Nanamma, knew that he had even returned to the village. The mango tree was in the middle of the fields, surrounded by dense coconut trees and sugar cane. He remained there alone until the farmhands got back to the farm around midday.

My father knew the rhythms of the village well enough to ensure that no one was there to stop him. It is likely that the poison caused his body to go into violent spasms for several minutes because his body, hands, legs, and neck had cuts and scratched from kicking dirt, rocks, and twigs on the ground around him. His clothes were torn in places, his face was swollen, darkened, his mouth was frothing and his eyes bulging. Unfortunately, I think it must have been an agonizing end, and I thought he must not have known it would be so violent.

He was found like that, under the tree, the tin container kicked away from his body. His dog was crying by his side, restlessly running around. Suraya, our farm hand returned to water the animals and Jimmy ran to him, and kept running back towards the mango tree, barking loudly, and circling around. Suraya followed him to my father's dead body and in complete shock he immediately ran to the neighboring farm crying for help.

They called a doctor, but it was too late. Within minutes the news had spread through the village. People began congregating at the farm and the house. An hour later they brought his dead body home.

I could not understand why my father did this. I had known him as a strong-willed, warm, fun-loving person. Yet he killed himself in a brutal, appalling manner, leaving his family to suffer the consequences. I thought that one must have to have reached the limits of desperation to commit suicide. There were rumors that he was broke and killed himself out of shame. The absence of open conversation by my family about the death and particularly the lack of direct communication to me, his son, about what had happened made it clear that this was to be a taboo subject.

I knew we weren't wealthy like other branches of the family, but I would have not known if we were broke. If we were, my parents did a great job of hiding it. We had always been treated as if we were wealthy coastal farmers, which was certainly the image my father wanted to project. To the average Indian my father and mother gave the distinct impression they were wealthy. Most of my entire extended family seemed to be. But the reality was that my family's income was rather limited, even though they had the lands and the home for assets. Most had simply accepted their situation and learned to live within their means. Some had tried their luck at different business ventures, or trades. A few succeeded, but most did not. Those who were unwilling to adjust had to sell parts of their holdings to support their lifestyle.

Late one evening shortly after his death, I overheard a conversation between my mother and Lakshmi Pinni[4] her youngest and closest sister, about what my father had done. My mother said that my father had been depressed for months. Other than the movie theater, none of his businesses were going as he'd expected.

He had some conflict with his extended family because they disapproved of his financial decisions, risk-seeking, and "flashy" lifestyle. He had been respected for his no-nonsense attitude, so he was never confronted directly. But people talked behind his back.

---

[4] *Pinni,* aunt in Telugu

He was losing money. His transportation business had recently failed due to rising costs and reduced demand, and he had to sell it at a loss. His poultry business was beginning to improve, but the theater wasn't generating any big profits yet. His land holdings were the only thing that kept the household running.

He had borrowed money to start his businesses, the interest rates of local private money lenders that financed small business loans were a criminally high 24%. Even the nationalized banks in India charged 12-15% interest. It was extremely difficult to secure business financing from the national banks, given the overwhelming amount of paperwork they required. Because of the situation it was common for rural property owners to get financing through private lenders.

But the farmland did not make enough to service the loans and he had already sold some of the land a few years earlier. One of the money lenders, who happened to be related, spoke ill of my father behind his back when he questioned the compound interest levied, much higher than what was initially agreed on. He then refused to extend the loan period. Upset by the situation and against my father's wishes, my mother sold some of her inherited land to repay the loans. My father agreed out of pride and desperation. He had to endure the relative's taunts, greed and disrespectful behavior and then having to sell his wife's property was almost too much.

For families whose identity and wealth are based on the traditional landowning system, having to sell pieces of land and potentially end up landless is a real concern and a practical reality not taken lightly. The land was their source of livelihood and land ownership was the principal source of wealth. Our family's land had not come through the graces of some ruler or a get rich quick scheme, but was the result of previous generations' ingenuity, hard work and thrift. Having to part with such an important economic asset and family heritage due to poor choices was a painful and dislocating development.

India's conservative society and the family's risk averse elders would not be happy with such situations, often saying that families bring things like this on themselves. Potentially being landless is the worst thing for families in this situation. My father's money problems deeply affected his self-image, and his sense of confidence was shaken. To make matters worse, my father's older brother, a successful farmer, who fell out with the family over financial matters, spoke ill of my father, his spending habits, business debt, and even supported the relative who had publicly insulted my father.

When word of the criticism reached my father, it hurt him deeply that his own brother would speak against him publicly in that tightly knit village environment. When I heard about this, I felt real disdain for the relative who had lent my father money and who later swindled him simply out of greed.

I vowed not to associate with that relative and never to get in trouble over debt. Krishna uncle's views on debt made practical sense. Although I did take on debt at critical junctures, with all of this I developed an innate fear of debt and high interest offers; what happened to my father always stuck in my mind. Living within my means has been a lifelong obsession for me.

Surprisingly, I did not feel any anger towards my father's older brother. I always respected him and felt warmly towards him, just as my father had. The brothers had a complicated relationship and were not on speaking terms for a few years after disputes over their inheritance. But when his brother's son was of marriage age, my father enthusiastically spearheaded those efforts: arranging the marriage, communicating with the bride's family on his nephew's and the family's behalf, and taking responsibility for the wedding arrangements, ensuring everything was done properly. His differences with his brother did not impact his sense of responsibility towards his nephew and the family. The complexity of family relationships and those related dynamics never cease to amaze me.

My father dreamed of expanding into other businesses but was hindered by lack of funds and felt trapped. It did not help that he was free with money, spending it liberally on the people in his life. He was well known for socializing with family and friends and helping the needy by donating to various community causes. All this spending clearly outpaced his income, which brought him to the point of having to gradually liquidate assets.

In addition, the sporadic loss of personal relationships and respect from his extended family had a significant impact on his feelings of value and self-worth. He was a proud man and couldn't handle that exposure. He must have lived with a sense of failure and disillusionment. Before he committed suicide, he started experiencing bouts of depression and his social drinking habit mushroomed into cycles of binge drinking, to drown out his sorrows and escape some of his troubles. He feared that his financial situation would continue to deteriorate.

During one of these periods when his demons overwhelmed him, he had told my mother he did not want to live anymore. When this wave of depression passed somewhat, as they did, he was his charming self again. Whenever those dark periods resurfaced, he would emotionally sink and was clearly battling overwhelming anxiety, stress, and depression. The reality was that he was suffering from significant, seemingly uncontrollable mood swings which led him to drink more. This problem stayed with him and was likely a contributing factor in his suicide.

After hearing my mother describe this and then remembering what had happened a few months earlier the bigger picture was starting to come into focus, even for a child. I now could see that during my visit the previous summer he was going through one of his downswings. One night he was doing very badly, so my sisters were taken to the neighboring relative's house, and I was put on a cot in the courtyard since I had already fallen asleep early.

Nanamma was away that night, but my father's aunt was there. Sometime late in the night, I woke up to raised voices. My father was talking to his aunt and my mother was sobbing quietly, by the side of my cot. I heard my father say, "My children will be better off without me than with me. I am sure of that. I cannot ruin their futures doing what I am doing."

His aunt was trying to calm him down and told him to think of his family. I was tossing in my bed, my mother tried to help me to stay still, pulling me closer to her.

I've pieced it all together more clearly now. It hadn't occurred to me earlier when my father had visited me in the city and had those closed-door conversations with Krishna uncle and Satya auntie. What happened at the time of his death makes more sense when I see things now as an adult. As a child I understood only parts. My father was significantly depressed again. He worried the family would be ruined if his business and personal choices lead to financial collapse. He killed himself, believing he was not successful. He feared the worst and gave up.

Perhaps it was the easier thing to do. If life is a battle, he felt that he had lost. No one around him understood the reason for it or the depth of his despair. He had lost balance in his life. In his mind he was choosing his children's future over his own life, a false choice, and, I think, an unjustified act.

"My children will be better off without me than with me." The unforgettable feeling of that statement is never far from my mind. I could not understand how he could have thought like that. It led me to some unanswerable questions: "What sort of strength or courage is required to take one's own life?" and, "Is it strength or weakness, is it courage or cowardice, is it sacrifice or selfishness?" or "Did he hate himself and his life so much that he had to kill himself?"

To my surprise he had spoken to several people about his state of mind and how he was feeling, but they hadn't done anything. Maybe no one knew enough to do anything about it. Mental health is still largely a taboo subject in India, and this often leaves people with few options when they are in crisis. This is a big difference from the western world where it is a much more accepted topic. I don't know that had my father and my family not been trapped in a traditional mindset, would he have gotten help? Then I began to wonder if the fault was not with my father but maybe my family. "Did he fail his family, or did his family fail him?" and "Why wouldn't his love for his family pull him back from the brink?"

I think in the end no one really understood or knew him or his inner workings well. He kept everything hidden behind a strong extroverted personality. I always felt it was important that he chose to see me at the end, spending his last few days with me. But I wondered, "Why would he choose to do that?" For all intents and purposes, I was the last person he ever really spoke to, and he didn't say much. Realizing this, I started feeling an enormous cloud engulfing me. I had been given so much responsibility from my now dead father, and the burden of that choice weighed on me. I began to worry, "What if I don't live up to his expectations?" With many questions but few answers, I've spent sleepless nights worrying about my promise to him.

By the twelfth day of the death ceremonies, most of the relatives had left. Lakshmi Pinni stayed for a few extra days to support my mother. I insisted on staying with my mother and sisters, unwilling to go back to the city. My father had made me promise I would take care of the family. That responsibility was mine now.

The family elders were split on what should be done. Some sided with me, but others including Krishna uncle, disagreed vehemently. He felt that my admission to the new school gave me the best shot at a promising future and was what my father wanted all along. My mother agreed with my uncle, although she was desperate to keep me home. She could not stop crying, but she insisted I go to school. She asked me to complete the academic year, promising to revisit the situation the following summer.

My mother's father, Rao Tatha was a well-to-do landowner from a nearby village. He and his four wealthy brothers were community leaders; it felt like they owned half the village, **one uncle was the village president, and another was the village secretary.** Over the years our family had built the temple, the school. They lived in a large residential compound, reminiscent of the traditional South Indian house. Rao Tatha was known for his generosity and affability. He was a lavish spender. He had the first car, motorcycle, telephone, and other modern conveniences in the village.

Rao Tatha tried to convince my mother to move back to his village, where she and my sisters would be more comfortable under his care, rather than let them struggle where they were. She refused; she didn't want to make any changes. She argued that her life was where her husband had been and that she would make it on her own with the resources she had. Rao Tatha was unconvinced, but he relented.

# 3

## Having To Go On

**LOST IDENTITY**
**NOVEMBER 1983**

I RETURNED TO THE CITY with Krishna uncle and Satya auntie the day after my father's funeral, and I was sent directly to school. As might be expected I was not ready, but no one seemed to care. I started feeling lonely, shaken. Until then I had been the privileged one and the source of everyone's pride and I was equally proud of my family. But now I felt like a loser, from a family of losers, whose father had killed himself. These guilt-ridden thoughts affected my morale and my confidence. My formerly boisterous personality disappeared. The proud son of an energetic man was now the shamed son of a man who committed suicide.

As I walked through the playground, two of my best friends ran towards me and hugged me. "Sorry to hear about your father. We heard that he passed away in an accident. We had no way to contact you. We are all so sad for you," one of them said. "In an accident?" Without saying anything, I kept walking, staring at the ground just shaking my head, nodding yes and no to most of their questions.

We arrived at class together. Once the teacher arrived, she took the rollcall and told us there would be midterms in two weeks. She signaled for me to come to her desk and calmly inquired how I was feeling, and how my mother and sisters were doing. "I am aware your father died in an accident. You don't have to talk about it if you don't want to. But let me know if you need any help. I will make sure you get an update on all the lessons you've missed over the past two weeks."

I wanted to tell the truth, that he didn't die in an accident, that he killed himself. Dead by his own hand, dying in shame, leaving no one to care for his wife and children. I wanted to scream and cry, hug her and my friends, tell them all about how much everything hurt. But the news of him "dying in an accident" seemed easy. As much of the truth as I wanted to tell, it felt dishonorable at the same time. I wondered, "Will some of my friends think less of me if I told them the truth?" That was my biggest fear.

So, an agreeable lie was spread about my father's death. I maintained the lie. Perhaps a bit of dignity is what one seeks, even from death, no matter the nature of the death. There wasn't even anyone for me to speak to in the first place. Everyone wanted to avoid the issue at school and at home. It seemed they all knew, but no one wanted to talk. When they did, it was quietly behind my back.

My teacher wanted to help, but I wasn't comfortable speaking with her about it, nor could I speak with Satya auntie or any of the cousins. Krishna uncle did not want to engage in any such touchy-feely matters. Going to school, studying hard, getting good grades was all that mattered to him. But I felt my life was a big lie, and I was a phony by going along with it, and even more than that I started feeling the adults in my life were phony as well. A surge of quiet anger kept building inside me.

By then it was time for standard public exams, a statewide exam covering all subjects. This was the first standardized exam that students had to take on their way to college. I stood second statewide, out of

100,000 or so students, ranking first in many subjects, and missing first place by one point. My name and my father's name were on the front page of the newspapers, along with a short article on my academic achievements. It was a high point in my academic career. Having just lost my father, my small accomplishment made the entire family happy.

That summer, back in the village, I began seeing things in ways I hadn't before; my home, the village, the people, everything seemed different. Except the rosewood bed set, everything felt dilapidated: our home, the furnishings, appliances, and all my favorite spots. The oversized bank safe in the living room now repulsed me. It was one more sign of our lack of real status, for I knew it contained nothing of value. By that point I learned to know better, and I couldn't stand it. My mother was barely getting by.

Managing the poultry business was too much, so she shut it down. After my father's death, the movie theater's other partners kicked her out. She tried to get a little sympathy from the partners in hope of retaining the share or at least collect some value for the buyout. It was a commonly held belief in the village that without my father, there wouldn't have been a theater at all. I sat through the discussions silently, I saw first-hand how ruthless, and money-minded people can be. They were respectful to my mother and talked softly but they did nothing to help her out in any way at all.

My father had been very significant in the lives of the people around him; his voice mattered, his views mattered, his presence mattered, and he had an important place in the village. It felt that people cared a little less about our family and I wondered if the suicide made us less worthy in their eyes, or was it simply his absence? Or was it all just in my head? I did feel a sense of poetic justice when my father's ex-partners were forced to shut down the theater later. Most people said that my father had kept it together and the remaining partners could not manage to run it. It felt like my father was needed, after all.

A small group of his loyal friends stood by my mother and supported her. But she was unwilling to accept much beyond encouraging words, wanting to take care of things herself, although previously she had never had to sort out business finances or running the farm. She even refused help from her siblings and Rao Tatha, instead selling her jewelry, and taking expensive loans, but smartly repaying them as promptly as possible.

In the not-too-distant past, women in our families weren't educated or prepared to manage farms or businesses. When I was very young, I remember Nanamma's rickshaw with a screen covering it even if she was going to visit a neighbor a few blocks away. My family often told stories about how she was brought from her village after the wedding (in the early 1920's), carried by six to eight people in a palanquin style traveling chair, crossing thirty kilometers.

By the time my mother was married things had become more liberal. She traveled unscreened when she went to visit nearby. At home, at most she would do things with my father and with friends in the privacy of our house, but she wouldn't talk with other men, other than younger relatives, outside our home. She wouldn't even directly face my father's older brother or her father-in-law after her marriage, she would step out of the way, as a sign of respect in line with customs and traditions. It was some variation of what was called a "purdah or gosha" system, purdah meaning screen, gosha meaning seclusion. As time passed this practice has slowly waned, but back then it was still practiced by traditional families.

Traditionally after a husband's death, women remained in the home, wore white to signify their state as a widow, stopped wearing their bindi, bangles, and other expensive jewelry. Although my mother dressed very modestly without much jewelry, she did not wear white, nor did she sit at home after my father passed away. Unable to afford private transportation, she traveled by hired rickshaws, taxis, and city buses to do what she had to do. She would switch modes of transport many times to get from point A to B, waiting in dusty bus stops, along filthy roads, and sunburnt pavements.

Once I overheard her speaking with a cousin who inquired about her modest dressing and urged her to dress better, my mother said, "it is important for a young widow to dress and groom modestly to avoid **unwanted attention from opportunistic men.**" Even holding such conservative thoughts my mother still ventured out into the world on her own to protect and nurture her young family the best she could. People complained about my mother choosing to mind her affairs, commenting about her independence, traveling by bus and share-autos. Of course, she was not faced with abject poverty, or hard labor or any severe deprivation just to feed the children or make ends meet, and none of us had to endure an abusive childhood, but seeing my mother suffer that way, dress that way, mortgage her jewelry, and make personal sacrifices hurt me deeply and made me anxious at my inability to help.

After their husband's death women were expected to either depend on their parents or their in-law's family to manage their economic affairs and make decisions for them. They were to simply take care of the home. Had my mother chosen that route, my sisters would not have attended good schools, I wouldn't have had a real role in family decisions, and my mother would lack the freedom to make her own choices.

My mother was progressive in her thoughts. She had a desire to free herself of the shackles of such a traditional world.

After my father's death I kept hearing from those around me saying, "You are now the man of the house, you must do whatever it takes to uphold your family name and care for your mother and sisters as soon as you are able. You must study hard and make your family proud. Your father made a poor choice, but he sacrificed a lot for your family. Help your mother find peace." The weight of these responsibilities was enormous at twelve years old.

I started having a disturbing reoccurring dream around that time. I was a lone warrior wandering around deep forests on horseback searching for his kingdom. It kept me up and made me anxious. Every time I had the dream it would linger in my mind the entire next day. What did it mean? Frustrated, I started questioning my family's situation and how had it gotten to the point it had.

Why we weren't wealthy like our relatives? Three children must have ruined my father's finances and drove him to suicide. As much as I loved my mother, I drove her crazy by questioning why she had more than one child, why she was married off to my father and not someone wealthier, what were her parents' motivations? I even questioned their judgment, and of course, why my father had killed himself.

My mother recognized my frustrations but had no answers. I then moved on to questioning the other adults around me, which got me labeled a difficult child, someone who defied the family elders and wouldn't listen to anyone. In Indian society children were expected to remain silent and dutifully comply with the adults, and anything different was considered confrontational and disobedient.

Frustrated by my relentless pestering driven by my agony, one day my mother told me, apparently kidding but in a serious tone, that my two sisters were hers but that I was adopted, and they took pity on me when I was brought home from a foster. Thoroughly hurt, I walked out barefoot in the scorching summer heat. An hour later they found me two kilometers away, wandering aimlessly, and brought me home. It was as though I wanted to run away from the realities of my life.

At the end of summer break after my father's death, Krishna uncle knew I didn't want to return to the city, and that I had tried to convince my mother to stay home. Any earlier resistance I had about returning to school when my father was alive was seen as a child's tantrum and Krishna uncle did not mind that; but this was too much.

Maybe hearing about this from a relative upset him, or my father's absence made him feel more pressured. He was deeply offended by my lack of gratitude for what he and his family were doing for me. When I got to the city, he pointed his finger at me and warned me sternly to absolutely watch my step. "You are welcome here only because of your mother's plight and my commitment to your father. Or else I would have asked you to leave."

I now recognize his frustration because he had set aside his own needs and toiled to keep his word to my dead father to make me an upright educated good human being. It was as though my uncle was devastated after my father's death. His resolve to come through on his promise to my father became even stronger than ever, the restrictions he imposed on my activities became unbearable over time.

Satya auntie stood by, clearly upset, wiping away her tears, and unsuccessfully tried to calm Krishna uncle. I listened, deeply hurt, my anger increasing. I wanted to leave but couldn't without damaging my mother and her relationship with Krishna uncle and Satya auntie. Krishna uncle threatened to throw me out but took me back. I felt I was unwanted both by my mother and Krishna uncle. During this time, I stopped playing with my friends, all I wanted to do after school was finish my homework, sit in a small chair by the window, and stare into the sky. What I was thinking about, no one ever asked or seemed to care. I had become sort of a sad little adult.

I felt betrayed. Unable to express myself, my feelings toward my father started turning into anger and bitter resentment. Was he not the man I thought he was? Was he weak and sentimental? Did he die a loser? I wanted to rip up the Rs.100 bill he had given me at the train station, but I couldn't; so, I stuck it in a box and stashed it away, never touching it.

I became more introverted. Feeling lonely, self-doubt started creeping in, which I deflected with a hard outside shell, perhaps like my father had done to try to hide his own insecurities. I started getting into fistfights. This got me in trouble, of course. The suppressed anger I had towards my father, Krishna uncle, his family, their rules, and the chaotic environment of the home's close quarters, started manifesting in parts of my life. Perhaps because there was no way for my father to express his disappointment now that he wasn't around, I started rebelling at any perceived hostility from any of the people in the apartment, particularly my cousin Karthi Bava. There were physical confrontations, verbal arguments, thrown objects and passive-aggressive behavior was routine. Each day a new drama, either in the mornings or in the evenings. The only quiet time in the apartment was when I was at school.

Krishna uncle did not understand what was going on—honestly, neither did I. The family was upset about my new defiant attitude. His response did not help. I wanted out. I couldn't stand another day.

My new school had a policy for regular teacher parent conferences to review student performance. I told this to Krishna uncle, he misunderstood this as being summoned for some disciplinary problem. No amount of explaining that everything was fine could save me from an undeserved thrashing again. He never attended these meetings.

Another time, he tersely asked me again to leave after an argument over some act of disobedience. In a fit of rage, I yanked my suitcase from the top of a steel almirah, pulling down everything else stacked over it, grabbed whatever clothes I could, and stormed out. Satya auntie followed begging me to return, which I ultimately but reluctantly did. The situation and the relationships never seemed the same after that.

Deepa and Sasi came to Hyderabad for the first time during my eighth-grade year, not to visit me, but to participate in the wedding of Krishna uncle's third son. They stayed with us for four days. As I watched them interact with my friends from the city, for the first time I noticed how my sisters were not like the city children.

Attending the village school and living in a rural environment, they were different, not in a good way. They stood out. They looked rural. I had never noticed this when I spent time with them during my summer breaks. At home, in the village I was the one that was different, but it was a welcomed difference. It seemed like children in the village wanted to be like me. and.

When Deepa and Sasi watched how things in the household played out for me over those few days, the harsh tones, the critical comments, and so forth, it upset them. One evening they broke down, hugging me, crying inconsolably, they felt sorry for me, saying, "We don't know how you can live here. We are very sorry you were sent here. We couldn't live here if we were asked to, we would want to be home, we wish you could come with us."

Krishna uncle had purchased a small plot of three acres along the outskirts of the city and set up a poultry farm which his second son, Ramu Bava ran after he got married. I looked forward to visiting the farm and spending some weekends there in the company of Ramu Bava and his wife.

At my new school, I also became close to two friends who had lost parents around the same age. We were drawn together; I think we understood each other. Not much was ever directly shared or spoken, but we connected over our loss. Pain has a way of gravitating towards pain, seeking comfort from its companionship.

On my subsequent visits to the village, I would not go to our farm where my father had killed himself. I stayed home the whole time. My mother encouraged me to play with the other children or visit relatives. I didn't want to, so I refused. While Deepa and Sasi missed our father, they did not seem as broken and lost as I was. My mother's family was there to offer emotional and moral support, which may have made it easier for the girls to cope. My mother was a pious, spiritual woman, known for her friendly nature. She had a nurturing and comforting manner. No matter how difficult things got, she never let the girls know it, doing whatever was necessary to keep the family going.

A few weeks into my eighth-grade summer break, a little over a year after my father's death, I visited my cousins at a nearby village, Mudinepalli, a hundred kilometers away. I spent several days there with my aunt Saru Pinni, my mother's first cousin, and her husband, Raja Babai[5], a charismatic larger-than-life figure, and a prominent politician in the district.

They welcomed me warmly and I had the opportunity to get close to my cousins for the first time. In stark contrast to our village home and our situation, they seemed to be better off in every way. More importantly, Raja Babai seemed like the type of father figure I was missing. I found myself drawn to him and spent a significant time with him, tagging along with him on his daily routines. I don't really know how he saw me, although he always expressed a fondness towards me, but in my mind, I adopted him and the family as my own. I was desperate to find any stable family that I could call mine.

That was when I learned of a family story that Saru Pinni, also my father's first cousin, was initially expected to marry him. For some reason it did not work out, and my father ended up marrying my mother. As first cousins, my father, mother, and Saru Pinni and Raja Babai remained close.

---

[5] *Babai*, means uncle in Telugu

Their three children remained close to me, particularly their daughter Chinni Akka[6] and older son Venkat Anna[7]. My mother's other first cousin, Principal Mava[8], owned and administered an English language school for day and boarding students in that same village. Raja Babai's children attended the school along with several others from the extended family. I fell in love with everything about Mudinepalli.

However, when Krishna uncle found out about my summer visit with Raja Babai's family, he warned me sternly not to socialize with them, saying they were a wealthy political family and my friendship with them and my relationship with Raja Babai wouldn't serve me well, and I would get spoiled and start feeling entitled to their level of privilege and comfort. I disagreed with Krishna uncle, and we exchanged some words over it. For years after, he was skeptical of my closeness to those cousins.

Although I was only a couple of years older than Deepa and Sasi, the events in my family and my consequent relationship with them created an uncommon amount of responsibility for someone my age. My promise to my father always lingered in the back of my mind. Combined with my thoughts about their visit to Hyderabad earlier that year and my interactions with my other cousins and children from Principal Mava's school, compared to other girls their age I realized they lacked opportunities and were falling behind. I started thinking about why the girls should go to an English convent school, like I had. But it wasn't my decision. Everyone in the family always said, "Girls don't need such a fancy education. What will they do with it? They will marry and tend a home eventually. Local schooling is sufficient for that." I disagreed, having seen what was possible, observing other independent women in the city, my teachers and some of my friends' mothers who were professional, and career oriented. My sisters could do better given the same opportunities.

Getting my sisters out of the village was in their best interest and really served everyone's purposes. Why not move them to the city? My

---

[6] *Akka*, means elder sister in Telugu
[7] *Anna*, means elder brother in Telugu
[8] *Mava*, means maternal uncle in Telugu

mother could rent a small house and we could live together as a family. I always wanted to be with my family because, as far as I figure it, I was sent away too young. I now see that a lot of the ideas I had as "plans" for my sisters were more aspirational hopes to be reunited with my family. When I told my mother again about the idea of taking everyone to the city, she said, "While there is nothing better than all of us together, we cannot afford a decent life in the city. On top of that, I'm not comfortable being in the city, I'm used to village life."

During my ninth-grade year, my grades started to suffer. The emotional stress kept me from concentrating on my studies and I was anxious all the time. I found myself pretending to read but lost in thoughts with a certain amount of confusion and distress. That year I was third in my class. I imagined Krishna uncle hitting the roof and the cane in the corner breaking in half across my backside. Third in class! He might just kick me out.

To avoid the consequences of this catastrophe, I looked for a way out. Thinking if I was sick or injured, he might let up, breaking my arm, or cutting my wrist were possibilities, but I couldn't cause possible permanent damage; it had to be something I could recover from quickly.

Recently one of my friends had been hospitalized for conjunctivitis, that evening a plan came to me. If I couldn't catch the real conjunctivitis, I would create it. I ground red crayons and filled my eyelids with the powder. I woke up mildly feverish, with swollen red eyes, I could hardly see. They were worried, but Krishna uncle was rushing to work and told me to go see the eye doctor. While he laced his shoes, I handed him my report card, wiping my watering eyes. He glanced at it, shook his head, and signed it, with a disappointed look, but without uttering a word. For a moment, it felt like he'd figured out my scheme. But the way he shook his head he looked as if he was ambivalent. I was relieved for a moment, but it bothered me that he acted as though he didn't care anymore. I felt like a disappointment.

Nevertheless, I walked to the eye clinic and explained to the attendant outside that I needed to see the doctor right away. The doctor took one look at me and said, "You must tell me what you did so I can treat you. If you don't, I will tell your uncle that you are faking being sick." I still feigned ignorance. Shaking his head, unwilling to believe me, the doctor washed both my eyes with a soft cleansing fluid and prescribed a soothing eye ointment. I ran and grabbed my report card from home and rushed to school, pleased with myself for having pulled off my scheme.

Around the same time, it had been decided by Krishna uncle that I would be an engineer; it was seen as a safe bet for middle-class children. "At a minimum, you can earn a decent living as an engineer. But after graduation I want you to qualify for the Indian Civil Services, that is my dream for you," he told me. Raising someone who passed the rigorous Civil Services exams and rose in the prestigious Indian Administration Service would be his best legacy, he felt.

I didn't have much choice, and I wasn't rebellious enough to say "no." Questions like, "What are you good at?" or "What makes you happy?" did not matter. Playing it safe is the middle-class Indian way. We were not to be passionate about anything, but practical at everything. But I knew I didn't have the aptitude to even hang a picture frame correctly, for heavens' sake, and I was to be an engineer? But as the saying goes, fake it till you make it.

While I desperately wanted to get out of Krishna uncle's home in the city, my mother insisted I stay until I finished school, then go away to college. I was trapped like a caged animal, restless, and suffocating. And although unable to fix my situation, I managed to help the girls when I returned to the village the following summer.

.    .    .

## WOMEN ON THE MOVE
## SUMMER 1986

During the summer after ninth grade, Principal Mava happened to visit us at Vundrajavaram. By then I knew his English medium school had an excellent reputation, on par with the convent school in Tanuku, and was far superior to the Telugu medium village public school the girls attended. Since my mother kept refusing to move to Hyderabad, I took a chance.

When Mother went inside the kitchen, I snuck into a conversation with Principal Mava as he sat chatting with Nanamma. I shared my views about moving our family to Mudinepalli at least so that Deepa and Sasi could get educated there with him, and how my mother refused to listen, citing financial reasons. He agreed with me, it would be important for the girls. Nanamma admonished me, hushing me to stay silent and not get into adult subjects.

The unpleasant and not necessarily healthy reality was that because of my father's suicide I felt compelled to take an adult role in my family's life. My mother never required it of me, choosing her own path instead. But I was impatient with my own rebellious thoughts that demanded quicker change and more action. And until I got the answer I wanted, I learned to push my desires, often frustrating my mother. In this way I had to grow up very fast.

Before I could say anything further, Principal Mava said, just as my mother came into the room, he could offer my sisters admissions to his school at a discounted tuition. "I have great regard for you as my cousin, and I always liked these two sweet girls. I wish more could be done for them, but I cannot waive the fees entirely as we have costs to bear. Please think about it, if it is possible to pay the reduced tuition, you may take me up on my offer at any time." Once Principal Mava left, I started telling my mother this was the best opportunity for the girls. But she wasn't keen on sending the girls away to a boarding school, even one operated by her cousin.

Rural families believed that girls were best protected at home in the parents' care and sent them to local schools. The abuse and violence in Indian towns and villages generally revolved around property, politics, caste, religion, and women. Gandhi famously said that India and Indians could truly claim independence only when the women of the nation could freely walk the streets at midnight.

That has yet to happen, and women's dignity, independence, and safety is an issue India has been grappling with. Indian women learn to unfortunately live with the cat calling, wolf whistling, lewd remarks, obscene gestures, and harassment in their daily public life. So wherever possible, women from traditional families are generally accompanied by a member of the family or a friend or encouraged to travel in twos. Though it was common for boys to be sent away to boarding schools, it was not the same for girls. Those who were interested in better education for their girls relocated entirely. Other girls simply dropped out of the system after high school.

Given the situation, the only way for Deepa and Sasi to go to Principal Mava's school was if the whole family moved to Mudinepalli and rented a home there. I kept pushing my mother. She agreed to consider a move, I think to get me off her back, reasoning that they couldn't move that year in such haste anyway. The girls were excited about joining the new English medium school in a new place. This move also had the added benefit of being closer to Raja Babai and my cousins. I was worried that my mother was just trying to appease me, with no intention of following through, so I made her promise to keep her word. I left for the city at the end of summer break excited about the new prospects for my family.

In tenth grade exams are given to determine your fate for higher education and career placements. Everyone, other than Krishna uncle, expected me to repeat my earlier excellent performance. Although my grades only dropped to third in the class, I felt like a failure and Krishna uncle was coming down on me harder, often saying that I was giving him a bad name and that I needed to be set straight.

Until that point my success had been fueled by a sense of purpose driven by my father's wishes, but his absence left me lost. My sense of purpose was missing. I did not do well on my tenth-grade exams, even though I was second in school. Something had changed, and I'd stopped caring about my academic performance. During the tenth grade, my mother finally decided to move from the village to be near her cousin's school, saving on housing expenses by taking care of a vacant home, as suggested by Lakshmi Pinni.

Leaving Nanamma behind was a hard decision, but my mother was becoming known as a capable widow, minding her family's affairs, and fulfilling her responsibilities, which unfortunately requires unpleasant choices. She was fearful of gossip from my father's family, that she was not taking care of her mother-in-law now that my father was gone. Only she knew how much she cared for Nanamma, always treating her as she would her own mother.

Family still lies at the heart of the Indian life. In traditional families, the grandparents chose who they wanted to stay with. Whoever they chose to be with saw it as an honor, a seal of approval. It's a mutual demonstration of love and bonding. It wasn't only for financial reasons. Nanamma had her own assets and could have lived independently if she wanted to. But an older person living on their own without the assistance of their children was considered a failure of sorts. That wasn't the situation at our home, since there was love and affection between Nanamma and the whole family. Nanamma had loved her son, my father, the most and chose to stay with us.

After my father's death Nanamma was terrified of parting with my sisters and mother during her old age. It was agonizing for both Nanamma and my mother, now that my mother was seriously considering a move; they both knew the decision was right for the girls' education. Given how entrenched in the village our family was Nanamma refused to move. My mother felt she would be going against her deceased husband's wishes and that he would have disapproved. Worried about Nanamma's well-being, even Satya auntie urged her not to move. Fearing that she may somehow change her mind, I kept writing to her asking she not renege on her word, arguing that nothing else mattered as much as the girls' education.

In the end my mother was unable to make up her mind, and eventually went to the village shaman who invoked father's spirit, so she could speak with him directly. Apparently, during the conversation, he consented to the move. My mother desperately wanted to believe this and so set aside her rationality for practicality. Such was her devotion to my father's wishes, that despite the heartbreak he had caused she still needed his approval.

Sasi and Deepa had been pleading with Nanamma to move in with them. In a last-ditch effort I approached Nanamma and begged her to move, she listened but didn't change her mind. As a compromise, she agreed to go stay with her eldest daughter. That settled things to some extent and gave mother and the girls a better situation.

In the summer of 1987, they moved to Mudinepalli to attend the English middle and high school. Three years later they moved again to Eluru for undergraduate degrees at university. My mother was away from Vundrajavaram six years for my sisters' education before returning home.

It seemed a somewhat strange position for our family to find itself in. Twelve years earlier my father had separated me from the family, hoping to improve my future. After his death my mother made an even more difficult decision to keep me in the city, in order to honor his wishes. Now we were separating the family again to improve my sisters' future. Namamma lived with her eldest daughter, but passed away heartbroken, less than two years later. The family had worried about my mother being widowed so young. However, it seemed to make her stronger and more resolute, allowing her to weather the tough choices required for a better future for her children.

Once my mother finalized her plans to move away from the village, I started making plans of my own while I was in Hyderabad during tenth grade. Although the junior college offering the eleventh and twelfth grades was affiliated with our high school, the competition to secure the few seats required everyone to take a separate exam after tenth grade to determine entrance based on the results of the exam. Defying Krishna uncle's direction, I refused to apply to junior college and take the entrance exam. I wanted to leave Hyderabad, as quickly as possible intending never to return. I thought I could attend Principal Mava's school with my sisters in Mudinepalli, and we could live as a family. There was a huge argument about this when I announced my decision at the last minute and left Hyderabad after my tenth-grade public exams, but they could do nothing about it.

When I arrived in the village and told my mother what I had done, she was furious and disappointed by my apparent poor choice. She refused to talk except to plead with me to return to Hyderabad. As far as she was concerned, my entire pre-university education until junior college was meant to be under Krishna uncle's guidance and supervision. I spent the four or five weeks of summer vacation visiting my cousins and asking my aunts and uncles to convince my mother to allow me to stay with her. She wouldn't listen to anyone.

Towards the end of the summer break, she compelled me to honor my father's wishes for my education and brought me to Hyderabad. She knew that Krishna uncle would need some convincing to allow me back into his home, especially given how arrogantly I left.

As expected, Krishna uncle wasn't particularly open to the idea and made it clear that I was not welcome there any longer. My mother pleaded with him, she reminded him of his promise and urged him to forgive my actions as a teenager's hot headedness. After a lot of convincing by my mother and Satya auntie, who was happy and relieved to see me, my uncle relented.

The only problem was admission to junior college, I had not taken the mandatory entrance exam. Krishna uncle left it up to me to find a way to gain admission into that college or get admitted into a less desirable college and still pursue my schooling. Since it was my doing, I was to reap what I had sown, was his message. As much as I hated being back in the city, I hated having to go to a second-rate college even more. After a lot of feeling sorry for myself, the following day, I approached Brother John, the head of my school and who knew me personally. I explained my situation and my mistake in not applying for the admission or taking the entrance exam. He reprimanded me but also took pity on me. With Brother John's help, the junior college admitted me based on my existing credentials, overlooking the entrance examination requirement.

I went and did well in both eleventh and twelfth grades, although nowhere close to what people had expected of me, but still graduating with honors. Krishna uncle always chided anyone that got ahead through the back door, particularly when it came to securing college admissions with bribes to medical, engineering, or law universities. But it was a common practice in India, when only a few thousand engineering admissions were available through a common entrance examination, often taken by over 100,000 applicants.

He always said one needed to get ahead on merit and talent and not money. He strongly believed that success is to be cherished when it is achieved through ambition, talent, and opportunity, but only by fair means. He encouraged me to compare myself with others for individual excellence and not engage in unhealthy competition and negative comparisons with those that may seem more successful. He called it "Compiex": compare and compete for individual excellence in a positive spirit without any negativity.

He often said while I was blessed with intelligence and emotional balance, a superior IQ and EQ, I would only achieve success through my ability to be persistent, PQ, in the face of failure at some point in my life. He said the combination of these three factors was the secret to success and he called it PIEQ. My challenge during those two years was to get admitted into an engineering college based on merit, not one that would require my mother to raise money by selling some of the remaining land to give a donation to a private college.

Although I stayed in Hyderabad at my uncle's home for the next two years, my relationships were more strained than ever before, not just with my uncle but with my cousins as well. It was like living with strangers. The rest of the family saw me as the ungrateful, headstrong kid that didn't belong there. But because of their regard for my father and commitment to my mother, they were stuck with me. Satya auntie was frustrated because she could not convince me to temper my behavior or persuade her family to be considerate of my situation. It was like the Cold War at home, no big battles but lots of almost daily skirmishes.

My heart and mind were fixated on being with my family. I felt like I was jailed, and I longed to be released. Sometimes it felt like I was an unwanted pet, a cuddly puppy the family brought home earlier without much thought but became overwhelmed by the unruly dog it grew into, and then not knowing how to handle it. They were unwilling to let me go and suffer some unknown fate, but equally difficult to keep at home and care for me.

Their frustrations manifested themselves in increasingly harsh treatment; this was only amplified by my rebellious, unflinchingly arrogant pushback. I simply kept going through one day at a time, thinking of my mother not wanting to cause her any more grief, I remained committed to finishing junior college. My only source of respite was my two close school friends who I spent most of my time with as well as the lengthy letters back and forth to Chinni Akka.

In 1991 two years after I left his home Krishna uncle turned sixty and retired from his government position. Using some of his retirement savings, he had finally managed to build his own home on the outskirts of the city close to his son's poultry farm. Fearing negativity from them, I had avoided visiting them after leaving for engineering college, when he invited me to his new home. I went reluctantly, pressured by my mother to attend and that I would be disrespecting my uncle if I didn't attend.

I was moved by the warmth shown to me by my cousins, who were more than happy to see me. It was as though all the earlier years of meanness pointedly targeted at me was to serve a larger purpose and that purpose was fulfilled now, at least in their minds. Everyone hugged me, my auntie wiping away happy tears, and my uncle playfully chided me for staying away for so long. When I looked around the new house, I saw that auntie had put on display all the medals and awards I had received during my school years in a cabinet adjacent to family photos. The only non-nuclear-family picture was a photo of my father.

My auntie and uncle loved and respected my father, and I always appreciated that. Although Krishna uncle expressed his disappointment that I didn't attend a better engineering college, he reminded me I could still find redemption by qualifying for the civil services exam. Everyone expressed pride in what I had achieved and my future potential as an engineer, while teasing me for all the trouble I got into, and we all were able to laugh about it. It felt like I was, after all, a successful project for them.

To progress, one must be free. To be free, one must unshackle themselves in many ways. Only the liberated can act on their hopes. Hope and progress are the inseparable components of life, entwined with bold and timely actions. Although my father couldn't free himself from the village, I believe moving away from the village to seek better educational opportunities for her daughters helped free my mother from family expectations and traditional responsibilities. Unlike my father's earlier decision regarding my education, while serving the single-minded purpose of giving me the best possible professional opportunities, it left me needing emotional fulfilment. This remained with me for my whole life. My mother's decision to move made a big difference in my sisters' lives, without sacrificing the emotional bonding they wanted with each other.

# PART II

## HAVING TO ACT THE ADULT

*You are made by your belief*
*As you believe*
*So you are.*

*– The Gita*

# 4

## Animal House and Other Acts of the Passionately Young

**DISCREET MATTERS**
**FALL 1990**

FOLLOWING KRISHNA UNCLE'S PLANS, during the summer of 1989, I secured admission based on academic merit to an engineering program in Vijayawada, 300 kilometers away. By then I was so desperate to get out of Hyderabad that I refused to entertain any ideas about remaining in the city or going anywhere else other than Vijayawada, no matter how good the college or the program. I knew that simply getting away from my uncle's rules, no matter how helpful they were in the long run, would give me my own sense of independence. I did not want to be away from my mother and the rest of my family either.

Unlike most of my friends that chose to move away from their homes and families to attend college and enjoy the new freedom it brings, I picked a college in this city because it was close to Mudinepalli, where my mother and sisters lived in while they attended school. I was more interested in staying close to my mother.

After they moved to Mudinepalli, I had spent the two previous summer breaks with them. Since Raja Babai's family lived there, I spent all my time with my cousins and got close to Chinni Akka, his daughter, whom I considered my God-sister. She was four years older than me, and we had started writing to each other three years earlier. They were lengthy letters in which we poured out our hearts about our whole lives. My relationship with Chinni Akka was very special.

During those dogged years of teenage confusion, desperation, and depression, when I was set on getting away from Hyderabad, she protected me and saved me from potentially making worse choices. But I was losing focus in school, losing respect for many of the adults around me. She listened to my woes, responding to my lengthy letters about my ambitions with thoughtful and encouraging letters, like a big-sister. She believed in me and had great hopes for my future.

When I expressed a sense of impatience about my family's life, she reminded me to plan carefully and not do anything in haste. We were very fond of each other and enjoyed spending time together. We also shared many common interests in books, movies, art, and architecture. She was the one person I knew would always be happy to get a new book from me. With a loud raspy voice and a rambunctious personality Chinni Akka was everyone's favorite and I was hers.

After finishing her undergraduate degree at college in Eluru, she married and moved to Vijayawada. So really part of going to college was because I wanted to be near her and that part of the family. Lakshmi Pinni also lived in Vijayawada as well as extended family on my mother's side. I saw it as a perfect opportunity to get close to the people I desperately missed the previous fourteen years.

Besides the family bonding I enjoyed during my stay in Vijayawada and the personal friendships I made with some of my classmates, the best thing I came away with from my four years at college was Meena, my wife. She was one year my junior, and we had grown up a few kilometers apart in Hyderabad without knowing it. And while we loved each other dearly, like other times in my life, I would find the demands and constraints of traditional Indian society at odds with my plans and the modern world.

Women in engineering colleges were uncommon at that time. Out of the 800 students on our campus, there were only about fifty women. As might be expected they were highly sought after by many of the male students. Anyone interested in befriending them had a lot of competition for their attention. Meena was beautiful, and luckily for me, someone from Hyderabad was friends with her family, so when she was accepted, they mentioned me as a possible contact there.

After arriving on campus, she sought me out. By then, I'd lightened up once again. Perhaps it was moving to Vijayawada, or leaving Hyderabad, or being closer to my family, I'm not sure, but I was relieved. College gave me a new sense of freedom; one I had craved since middle school.

In Vijayawada, I was as free as a bird. After cajoling my mother into buying me a scooter so I could get to college, I could go anywhere, watch any movie whenever I wanted to, stay up late, eat anything as I pleased. I felt independent for the first time in my life. I could simply live my life without someone else's oversight or restrictions.

I quickly developed a network of friends, a small coterie of fifteen strong. All of us were so close that we considered ourselves blood relatives, especially the group who moved to the U.S. one after the other. All these families remain close to this day and get together often, with our children sharing a common sense of familial bond strengthened by their parents' closeness in the U.S.

Early on in Meena's time at school, someone pointed me out to her, but she was not impressed and told me later all she saw was a guy with a loud voice, an even louder laugh, hanging out with the boys, who didn't seem particularly serious. Meena had watched me with my group of friends for a couple of days. Sitting under the vast tree canopy at our campus, our over-the-top antics ranged from "Animal House" to "American Pie," pranking each other, acting like idiots with a certain teenage crassness. This behavior did not make for a good first impression, and consequently she didn't look to me for advice or connections.

When I heard about her asking after me, my curiosity got the better of me, and I wanted to meet her. Our first meeting was casual, during a class break. But I couldn't keep my eyes off her, completely taken by her poise, my heart skipped a few beats, and her charm took my breath away. She was seventeen, I was nineteen. Her tall lean frame, sharply chiseled looks, olive skin tone, and greenish-hued eyes enchanted me. I decided to approach her.

We got to know each other a bit more with a group of common friends. We started spending time together alone, mostly under the guise of exchanging books. Soon the two of us were spending a lot of time together, discussing the books we read, along with movies, politics, music, as well as hopes and plans.

The more we talked, the more I loved her maturity, personality, the engaging conversations, her acumen, strong character, and her sense of initiative. She had a riveting personality, an imaginative mind, and what would start as a casual discussion often evolved into sharing personal matters like our problems, dreams, fears, family issues, life expectations. Our relative maturity was one of the things that drew us together. Before we were a romantic couple she became my best friend, I think that has a lot to do with the strength of our connection and commitment.

One day, I finally told her the truth about everything I had been hiding from everyone else in the world for so long. I told her about my father, the family, my sisters, and all the responsibilities I felt I owed to everyone. She understood and empathized with my whole situation. In turn, she shared her family's inner workings with me as well.

We had a lot in common. Our values were very much aligned, but we maintained distinct personalities as well as thoughts and solutions unique to each of us. I knew she liked me, simply because she was willing to spend so much time with me. One's ideas for the future can change after meeting someone like Meena. Mine did. Because of her I started getting more serious about my studies and where I really wanted to go.

The city we lived in, Vijayawada, was very conservative and to a certain extent everyone knew everyone within the close-knit circles, giving it the feeling of a village and not a city of 800,000 people. But those small social circles were a hot bed of gossip, just like a small village.

Maybe all Indians are villagers at heart; it's just the concept of who their village is that is important not necessarily geographic demographics.

The city was proud of itself, it had a long political and cultural history and was known for the quality of its schools and colleges. As a result, in addition to the locals, there was a whole community of academic migrants from neighboring villages looking for educational opportunities for students unavailable in rural areas.

In those days, the notion of platonic friendship between men and women wasn't common in India. People would view any association as a "love affair." At this time women generally didn't mingle socially with men even in colleges. Each had their own gender specific groups they moved with. Even non-sexual friendships were labeled romantic as little pieces of information made their way through the rumor mill. The women in this situation usually bore the brunt of the unpleasant consequences by having their reputations ruined.

We decided that we did not want to be talked about and went to great lengths to not be seen together, especially away from situations where there might be other men with competing interests. Even something as innocent as going to the same movie or restaurant at the same time seemed like a bad idea. We were trying to avoid any evidence of our association. We limited seeing each other to our homes, usually hers. It was not common for young women to have their own apartment. They would generally stay with relatives or in a dormitory. But Meena was unwilling to burden relatives and given the appalling nature of the dormitory she lived by herself, renting a cottage from an elderly couple.

Although most young people might not have taken such carefully calculated steps to be discreet it just seemed the only positive way forward for us. I think this shared secret amusingly served to bring us closer together because we were accomplices in our little conspiracy. When we were on campus, we even pretended we didn't know each other, at least not as close friends, but behaved as mere acquaintances.

It was very difficult and emotionally stressful to keep our relationship secret from even our closest friends. It would have been an unbelievable relief to be able to tell everyone, but the school was full of people with large egos and small minds and that's who we wanted to keep this information from. Despite our best efforts to maintain secrecy, a few rumors occasionally needed to be quashed and denied.

Regardless of how careful we were with our secret, a fellow student from college who knew Meena's grandparents, and therefore assumed the role of her self-appointed guardian, was offended by the rumor of our association. Without any solid evidence to add credibility to the rumors, he could not do much about it, nor could he muster the courage to confront me or Meena directly. Frustrated, he developed an animosity towards me and my friends and complained about Meena's college life and her associations with her family. They questioned Meena and were satisfied with her explanation of the situation.

Meena's family knew me and my friends by then and that helped convince them it was okay to be associated with us. We were somewhat lucky in this matter as families often forced their children to break away from such friendships between the opposite sexes, fearing further rumors. But Meena's family did no such thing, beyond cautioning her to be mindful of her reputation.

That year we decided to organize a picnic at a local beach. Meena, along with several of her girlfriends, had been at the beach the previous summer. When word of our picnic spread, the young man who knew her grandparents gathered some neighborhood bullies and threatened us with dire consequences if any of the women from the college were at our picnic. While this may sound far-fetched, this was not an uncommon situation in India. Schools, colleges, neighborhoods, in tightly knit communities often had trouble that ended in bloody brawls, physical violence or even abductions—sometimes with near-fatal consequences over disagreements regarding relationships between young men and women.

My friends panicked at this strange danger. None of my friends were aware of my association with Meena any more than others at college. A secret was a secret, and we kept it from even our closest friends, mainly to protect Meena's reputation. Although nothing was said outwardly, I knew the cause of this tension and was unwilling to jeopardize my friends' safety and security.

Together with a few others we decided not to back down but to seek the help of a Naval Base commander near the beach. My friend KP and I drove to the base a week before the picnic and asked to meet with the station commander. It was a crazy idea, but the commander agreed to talk with us. When he heard the threats being made against us and our friends and that we simply wanted a day at the beach, he generously decided to help. I think he felt bad for us, and he offered us access to the private beach on the Naval Base as well as the use of the base guesthouse. We kept all of this quiet, and no one outside our circle of friends knew what we had planned.

On the day of the picnic, about 45 people boarded a large tour bus and we made our way to the Naval Base. The rival group chased us on their motorcycles, taunting us along the entire two-hour drive. They planned to attack us and harass the women once we got to the beach. What they did not realize is that we out maneuvered them by getting to the Naval Base, which was off limits to them. Once we pulled into the heavily guarded base, they hung around the perimeter, then left having lost interest and tired from the two-hour chase.

As I said earlier, unfortunately it was not uncommon for college students to get into fights over minor matters, which is not so bright really. In fact, our class was the only group over a six year stretch at college, that graduated without any real fights with rival groups. To some extent we were lucky, and we stayed smart as well.

Years later, the student who knew Meena's grandparents ultimately realized he was acting immaturely. We recently reconnected and he expressed regret for his behavior. He felt ashamed of everything, having had an epiphany of sorts in his forties. I forgave him wholeheartedly; we were all young and stupid after all.

I lived with Lakshmi Pinni's family for college. That was home number three for me by then. I had a warm relationship with the large group of cousins and relatives who lived nearby. Living with cousins I was close to lessened my chronic homesickness and the need to be with my mother and sisters. I visited them during major holidays, or they visited me at Lakshmi Pinni's home during their holidays.

Vasu Babai, Lakshmi Pinni's husband, was an engineer who had set up his own factory and was the most welcoming person one could meet. Their home was always filled with visitors. I even had my own room. There were four large bedrooms, three full baths, huge living quarters, a kitchen with a garden balcony, all the modern amenities, multiple ACs, TV, telephone, refrigerator, a car. A full-time cook, chauffeur, watchman, as well as other servants were at Lakshmi Pinni's disposal, and there was never any food rationing. They had two children. Bobby, the youngest, was six years younger than me; we were fond of each other, and he looked up to me like an elder brother.

Living in that home I watched and learned the differences in family life as related to occupation, how the family's economic fortunes and basic outlook differed. My nuclear family was agriculturally based; Krishna uncle's family were civil servants and white collar oriented; and Vasu Babai's family was business focused. The common underlying condition that enabled the different families I looked at to flourish and lead a satisfactory life was *fiscal responsibility*, even as a matter of scale related to income and assets.

While my father spent more than he earned and always needed money, my uncle could not even earn enough salary for his needs, let alone have passive income from other businesses or land ownership and was short on money. Vasu Babai spent everything he earned and thereby never had money either. Though my natural propensity was to spend like my father, I was made to learn to be fiscally responsible, spending only within my income limits.

Another thing I realized was that agricultural families, workers' families, and business families had distinctly different risk appetites and the children that grew up within each of these economic environments behaved as articulated by their upbringing. I was fortunate for having experienced life under these three uniquely different family economic situations.

My family at home enjoyed getting updates about my college life. Just as I shared the details of many other elements of my life at college, I announced this captivating girl's arrival on campus, talking about her at every opportunity. I introduced Meena as my good friend to Chinni Akka and her husband, Bobby, some of my other close cousins, as well as my mother, Deepa, Sasi, and Lakshmi Pinni.

By then my mother and sisters had moved into a small rental house in a nearby town Eluru, about fifty kilometers away, where Deepa and Sasi were attending college. Meena liked my mother's peaceful, caring nature and she connected with my sisters as well. On their visits to Vijayawada, they would all hang out whenever possible. Deepa and Sasi developed a sense of appreciation for Meena's intellect, and her easy-going manner.

My family wasn't blind to the situation and soon they connected the dots, especially when I was on the phone so often, and sent lengthy letters to Meena, usually delivered by little Bobby. Every note we wrote teetered on the brink of demonstrating a romantic attraction towards each other, just stopping short of outrightly expressing our maturing feelings. But by then I knew I was in love. Our shared contacts from the city may have emboldened me, or Meena's open and friendly nature. It matched the prediction of an astrologer who once told Lakshmi Pinni that I was destined to marry a girl I fell in love with.

Although increasingly more common in India, "love marriages" weren't conventional, even with over a hundred Bollywood and other local movies being made on that subject annually. Indian movies generally took place in a fantasy world, not the real one. Any relationship where the bride and groom fall in love and marry for love, was labeled a "love marriage," and largely discouraged by society. This was due to their perceived impracticality and reputed higher failure rates versus "arranged marriages." In arranged marriages, it is expected that one eventually falls in love with the person they married after the marriage. The general thinking was that just as they learn to live with someone, they learn to love as well; believing that happiness is also in loving who you marry, and not only marrying who you love.

Even more radical than "love marriage" in terms of complexity was "inter" (fill in the blank) "marriage." Inter-class, inter-faith, inter-caste, inter-racial are some examples. Here falling in love was just the necessary first step. If that put you on a path of inter-something, life could get extremely complicated. Inter-somethings were not for the faint-hearted. Those were for either real progressives or the elopement kind of romantics.

People from conventional families, and who followed tradition, stayed away from messy marriages. It was much easier to get the family's blessing if it wasn't inter-something or was arranged by the families. Inter-faith marriage and inter-caste marriages were the most controversial, with caste being proprietary to the Indian culture.

The caste system in India is thousands of years old and rigid. If one digs deep, one finds historical explanations and reasons for its existence, but it is irrelevantly archaic now. However, its age-old effects persist even in everyday life. Therefore, inter-caste marriages were discouraged and looked down upon as a significant transgression of social norms. The poor bride and groom who pursued inter-caste marriage would have to fight a lifelong stigma, enduring everything to uphold their relationship.

Inter-class was a unique subset of this system. In India class was determined by a family's socio-economic standing. It was considered acceptable and advantageous for a family to marry up economically or otherwise, as though they'd just won the lottery. But for a family marrying down? That depended on all the reasons and factors that made the alliance desirable. Regardless of how the involved families felt, society had its way of viewing this and passing judgment, hotly debating who got the better end of the marriage.

Apart from this, any other form of inter-something marriage was rare. Given India's racial uniformity, inter-race wasn't as common, and largely manifested as an international marriage of some kind. As fairer skin is generally held in high esteem, any inter-racial or international marriage made to enhance the next generations' skin tone had an easier path to acceptance.

Within India, even interstate or interregional marriages aren't that common. Many cultural elements change dramatically in India, including language, customs, classifications, the states and regions, even between districts within states. Almost every 150 to 200 kilometers it's like being on another planet. Whatever the cultural uniformity brought India together as a nation does not apply when it comes to marriage.

One was expected to marry within the narrowest sub-segment of their heritage. But can one ever find a community not proud of its heritage and culture? So only having firsthand experience can one catch the subtle nuances of what was being negotiated. More than a billion people from the largest cities to the tiniest villages, seemingly united but isolated within their distinctive communities rarely truly intermingled.

I always wanted my marriage to be a personal choice not driven by tradition. Leaving it to someone else's judgment seemed inappropriate, like a sort of personal failure. I would argue with my family members about it over dinner all the time. They labeled me a rebel, and a lost cause in this matter. Meena had told me that the situation was more liberal at her home. Meena and I were swimming against the tide due to the stigma associated with love marriages, but we were willing to deal with it and put in the work because in the end we were very much in love. I will never forget how lucky we were to have found each other and make a life together.

A few months later, word of my association with a woman at college reached my cousin, Venkat Anna, Raja Babai's son. He was three years older, and I thought of him as a brother. Everyone admired his thoughtful nature and sought his advice. He was the one who had suggested I study Industrial Engineering for my undergraduate degree. Although my family had their suspicions about what was going on with Meena, no one had asked me directly. Venkat Anna confronted me one day about Meena, cautioning me and reminding me about my own looming family responsibilities: my two younger sisters' marriages, finding a job, getting settled and supporting my mother. He was concerned that getting distracted with girls might derail me. He asked, "Are you in love with her?"

"I like her, and we are good friends. I am not sure about much else and I have no idea how things may unfold," I said.

He advised me to stay away from that "sort of situation" and focus on my education, and not embarrass my family in any way. We discussed it at length sitting on the third-floor verandah of his large home, but we kept going in circles. Thankfully we finally reached a compromise.

"I will honor your request and not propose to her at any point. But I cannot reject her if she expresses her feelings to me." He seemed satisfied with that answer.

However, I had trouble letting go of something I wanted so badly. On this occasion Meena sensed my discomfort from my behavior with her after my conversation with my cousin and asked me if something was wrong. I dodged her questions, only telling her about my conversation with Venkat Anna but of course not the complete details. But given my indecisive behavior, she saw I was in a predicament. It was common for young lovers in India to pull back after having such "conversations" with their families. I was hoping Meena would muster the courage to express herself to me and save me from my quandary. But nothing happened.

Then, one day Meena called, asking to see me that evening. For the first time she asked me to take her on a scooter ride across the city, along the riverbank. That was where my wish came true. As we sat there along the moonlit riverbank under the stars Meena told me she loved me. She opened her heart and her feelings, saying she wanted to share her life with me. Any nervous doubts each of us had about the other's feelings were dispelled. Both of us couldn't have been happier.

When I asked what attracted her to me, she playfully teased, "You are the only guy on campus that wore good sneakers and spoke decent English." In ecstatic euphoria, my heart beat so fast that I could barely speak. The duty to my family weighed heavily in my thoughts at that moment.

Although I had shared many details with her earlier, I went over it again to make sure she was clear life may not be a bed of roses, but we would work towards a better future together. She understood, saying she was under no illusions. "Your deep sense of responsibility towards your family is one of the things that attracted me to you. If you can love your family so much, I am sure you would love my family the same way and that's very important to me. I'm sure we will be able to figure things out, and no matter what may come we can find a way forward, together."

Meena and I had almost two years to get to know each other to share our views on life, people, aspirations, and a real opportunity to make decisions about our lives. I knew Meena was the right person for me. I felt blessed for finding a partner that was enthusiastically helping with my responsibilities as her own and being my confidant and best friend. I was so glad she took the unorthodox action to make her feelings about me clear. When I asked about this, she told me she knew I would struggle with a decision and wanted to make sure at least her feelings were made clear. Thanks to her, my predicament was resolved to my utmost satisfaction.

Since childhood I'd been observing married couples around me and had begun to form an idea of who would be a "suitable wife" for me. I disliked marriages where the husband was the provider and "master," and the wife was subservient caretaker with varying degrees of submissiveness, depending on their personalities and relationship. Regardless of people's education levels or wealth, whether they lived in the city or in rural areas, this patriarchal power was a near-ubiquitous reality. Even in cases where the husband was a drunken fool, he was in charge, however badly. Wives generally would dutifully comply, mostly from cultural conditioning and from lack of other options.

The best matches I had seen were like-minded women paired with thoughtfully liberal husbands, I saw how those families flourished. My role models in this were Nanamma on my father's side, and my great grandmother, Devamma, on my mother's side. They managed their worlds quite well, commanding respect in a man's world, with a strong intellect and dignified aura. Seeing them made me realize that I wouldn't be content with the dutiful wife who was satisfied with a traditional role. I wanted an independent wife, just like them, someone to be a partner with, share the burdens and victories with and offer advice, a couple where each had equal status. The woman being completely her own person was the most important thing for me, and it was clear that Meena was the epitome of that.

Life got rather serious and busy after this. Meena still had over two years of college, and I had over a year. We decided to keep the relationship a secret from the world at large but would inform key people in our lives.

Meena first informed her younger sister, Radha, who she was very close to at the time and who I got to meet. Meena's mother came down to meet me from Hyderabad. She was the closest to Meena. A discerning, soft-spoken woman with a friendly smile and a positive outlook, she raised both her girls to be independent women. Besides the traditional mother-daughter connection, Meena shared a sisterly companionship with her mother, confiding in her desires, sorrows, joys, and fears.

We spoke at length over coffee, she made the customary inquiries about my education and my plans. We had met earlier during my short visits to Hyderabad, as one of Meena's many good friends. But this time it was different. She wanted to know me better and know more about my family. She had her own reservations about our family situation and the expectations my mother would have. She was worried my family's responsibilities would weigh down her daughter's future. However, Meena shared with me later that her mother was graceful enough not to express such concerns to me, instead, extending her full support to us.

The one condition she required was that we keep it private until we had both finished college. Our education was essential, and her daughter being independent was necessary to take any further steps. She was also concerned about Meena's father and grandparents' approval and wanted to disclose it to them only after I became "eligible," worthy of her daughter's hand. I needed a little clarity about my future, perhaps a job. That's when there could be a formal engagement, blessed by both families. Until then, it was to be a "friendship" to the outside world.

The concept of courting and dating over extended periods did not exist in traditional India. It's possible that she wanted to keep it quiet and give this secret and informal understanding a bit of time to see if our love fizzled away after its first blush, as many such romantic matters could.

Though I never doubted I would get my mother's approval, getting the rest of family's blessing was important. Every Indian family has the go-to person on major family matters. Depending on the need, these influencers have different roles, that of guide, mentor, counselor, confidante, guardian, advisor, an emergency financier, or simply a shoulder to lean on. Especially given that my mother was widowed, other family elders, uncles, aunts, had sway in most of our key family decisions.

Growing up in that environment, I observed many families handling their children's romantic matters in a way that mostly ended in break-ups because of their disapproval. Family elders generally meant well and only wanted what was best for their children but didn't always get it right. They all had certain expectations of the other's family, about their social, financial reputations, qualifications, appearance, and personality. I knew from the beginning that picking someone that met the right criteria would get the least resistance from the family.

In India most love birds kept their relationship a secret from their family as long as possible. When parents discover what is happening, it could lead to them hardening their stance over some legitimate concerns, as well as many imaginary exaggerated ones. This sometimes led to children being kicked out of the home or shunned into social isolation by their families. My goal was to eliminate every potential reason for a "no." That's exactly how it turned out.

My mother's chief concern was for my sisters' future if I was going to marry Meena. It was expected that men fulfill their family responsibilities before their own marriage. I assured her that she would have nothing to worry about, that I would still be there, and that no one was contemplating marriage anytime soon. I told her that I had this conversation with Meena already, so she was relieved.

Meena's family expected her to go to the U.S. for higher education, settle independently, and marry someone working there. Since my teen years, encouraged by Krishna uncle, my family thought that I should work for the Indian Civil Services. It was the highest-level bureaucratic role in India, a prestigious position everyone thought was within my reach given my academic aptitude. Initially, I entertained such aspirations as well, but realizing the short time I had to fulfill my family obligations, I changed my mind, because those positions have status but not salary, and one can't eat status.

Another unattractive option was to take employment in an underpaid work situation that was common in local Indian companies or bureaucracies, in locations reminiscent of mid-twentieth century workplaces with dingy, dimly lit, unclean surroundings. Minus a few successful large-scale enterprises in mega cities like Bombay, Bangalore, or Madras, the early 1990's India was still a relatively pre-global industrial consumer economy before world-class work culture had arrived, and I wasn't ready to sign up for employment in an unpleasant environment like that, even to get my career started.

One of the most successful industries in India is film making. The South Indian film industry was concentrated around Madras, a seven-hour train ride from Vijayawada. Like many teenagers I had long harbored a secret desire to be an actor, but I had not given it any serious thought. Successful actors were popular and wealthy. Given my desire to do something quick to settle down, without any real plan, on an impulse I decided to go to Madras during an extended break from school.

Meena wasn't aware of this trip because she was at her grandparent's during the break. Lucky for me, I ran into a small-time actor on the train who sat next to me, and we talked. He was in his late sixties with a tired look. During our conversation he told me about his early days, how competitive the field was and how he was deceived by people he trusted, which led him to lose bigger roles. He had been my age when he arrived in Madras and decided to stay rather than head home a failure.

I did not expect the industry to welcome me with the red carpet, but hearing his story made me think hard about the risks involved. He told me that at a minimum I would tough it out for a few years before I could expect to get decent roles in the movies. Anyone that doesn't get prime roles cannot expect to make much money. The message was that the odds are slim, but I could try my luck if I choose.

I didn't have much time to settle down, I could not afford to fail and live on scraps. I would need money to get my sisters married. When he learned I was about to complete my engineering degree, and possibly go to the U.S. for graduate school, he said I should turn back around and continue with that plan and let go of my unrealistic ideas about the movie business.

I reached Madras and wandered aimlessly for two days. I quietly returned home cured of the acting bug. Seeking higher education in the U.S. and emigrating seemed to be the best step forward. The stakes were high, it was time to put that theory to the test. So, aiming for this now seemed natural, especially for love.

A U.S. educated graduate was very alluring to the Indian middle-class and would quickly get family members' approval. A job there would hopefully help me earn enough money to have more independence and what better place to try our prospects than the new world? Both of us agreed the U.S. would improve our situation. We decided that I would prepare for the necessary exams, seek admission into a U.S. university, and Meena would follow me a year later after her graduation. But as they say, "The best laid plans of mice and men ..."

# 5

## First Steps Out the Door

**$300,000 — TO BE A MILLIONAIRE**
**SUMMER 1992**

EVEN PRIOR TO MY FATHER'S DEATH, my mother had to sell off some of the family's land to settle debts, pay for our education, and cover household expenses. So, after my father's death even the idea of me going to the U.S. was audacious. There was no way my mother could sponsor my U.S. education without selling some of the remaining land, but the income from that was critical for her and my sisters' survival.

My oldest sister Deepa was nineteen and in the final year of her three-year undergrad business degree. Rao Tatha and the family began considering her marriage, although neither my mother nor Deepa were in no rush. A relative suggested that Deepa's marriage be arranged with a cousin of ours, the son of my father's youngest sister. I vehemently opposed, feeling that he wasn't suitable. I was also against cousins marrying. Even though my parents were cousins, modern society needed more modern solutions, and I believed we should move away from these practices. But the elders disregarded my concerns for my sister and coerced my mother to agree to any arrangement proposed by the family elders.

To everyone's utter disbelief my father's sister's family made a counteroffer! They suggested we swap Deepa with Sasi, and that they'd be happy to have their son marry Sasi rather than Deepa. Sasi was the more outgoing of the two, with lighter skin while Deepa was quieter, with a darker complexion. It seemed that they were making a choice based on my sisters' exterior looks.

While the elders were disappointed, they were still receptive and tried to convince my mother. But when I heard about it, I was furious. I would not accept someone treating my sisters like that. I threatened to cut off anyone who continued with this terrible proposal and convinced my mother to not agree. Thankfully she did that as she was terribly upset as well and felt belittled. She reasoned they knew that Sasi was too young, only seventeen, and wasn't ready for marriage.

In a deft social maneuver, my aunt's family knew outright rejection of Deepa would upset everyone, but proposed Sasi instead of Deepa, knowing we would never accept it. They did not want Deepa, and if we were desperate enough to marry off Sasi instead, they would be happy to oblige. Now we would be responsible for rejecting the proposal. This is high level family politics and strategy, sort of crazy really. Deepa was disappointed, but not totally repulsed, at least not to the extent I expected. It must be her cultural conditioning which allowed her to react so casually, I thought.

It is also true, and part of my general objection to the whole system, that the son who was proposed, sadly became addicted to alcohol, gambling and lost his money and eventually taking his own life trying to kill his wife as well. While my heart went out to his situation, I shudder at the thought of my sisters being in her place, and spending years in an unhappy marriage. My mother moved on and was later instrumental in arranging this cousin's failed marriage while Deepa and Sasi always behaved as though the episode never even happened.

The dynamics of Indian family relations can still perplex me. I was the only one that could never forgive them. I never wanted that marriage to happen and was relieved when it didn't, but I felt my family were treated disrespectfully and that upset me more.

Anytime this type of situation arose, I wondered about the respect our family would have been granted had my father been alive. I wanted to restore respect for my family. This episode illustrated that it wasn't going to be easy and we needed to work hard for my sisters. That meant I had to get settled quickly and as well paid as possible.

When I vented about all this with Chinni Akka, seeing my desire to help with my sisters settlement and improve my family's reputation and my mother's lifestyle, she told me I was too young to worry about all those things. And I should live my life and focus on my education, and that caring for my sisters and minding their welfare was up to my mother.

"You are not their father, you are just one or two years older than your sisters, you should take care of your life," she said. I would hear none of it. Even as a teen, my impatience to get things in order the way I wanted was killing me. In my mind, these were my responsibilities and no one else.

My mother had fallen on hard times emotionally and financially. Her returns from the agricultural land she had leased out to a local farmer had been reduced to a measly $4,000, a far cry from the much higher income they had when my father was managing the larger farms and the businesses himself.

Agricultural income was and is tax free. India still was operating with many socialist economic principles, and senior government officials like Krishna uncle in Hyderabad did not have high salaries. By some standards, my mother was doing okay, even with her small income because she owned her home, the farmland, and she lived in an inexpensive city. But now I was asking for help to get an education in the U.S., the cost of which would truly stretch her limits. High costs aside, though, my mother was pleased with my plans.

Together with my college mate, Sarat who also aspired to study in the U.S., I started preparing for all the mandatory exams required of international students seeking U.S. college admissions. This required a visit to Bangalore, six hundred and fifty kilometers away to take an exam, and then Hyderabad later, to take another exam. It was customary for students in our position to try to find anyone who might be visiting from the U.S. and hit them up for information on colleges.

So once someone like me got wind of a U.S. returnee's whereabouts, it was important to do the best to try and meet with them directly. It was acceptable to request that they try to contact a specific university on my behalf to mail an application. International phone calls and postage was expensive, so we did anything to save a penny. Those travelers aided us in these efforts, maybe out of pity, or because it reminded them of their own similar struggles. They took the time to speak with us, sometimes while packing their bags for their return journey, stuffing them with all the free courier parcels they invariably got stuck with or while eating their final meal with their family.

The university application fees were around $50. I applied to five schools, carefully picking them, while Sarat did the same. Two of the five universities accepted me. The two top universities rejected me. The mid-range university placed me on a waitlist. My first choice from those that admitted me was Tennessee. It had a higher ranking for producing decent engineers, Eastern Michigan was my fallback option.

While I was trying to decide which school to go to, one of my network connections was a visitor from Michigan, who mentioned that he lived near Detroit. He told me, "It's an excellent place for mechanical or industrial engineering students, the schools there have a practical application-based curriculum. Students have a good chance of getting placed with the Big Three auto companies after graduation. A lot of the industry is in or around Detroit—it is the capital of the auto world." Going even further he said, "Going to school in a place where there may be jobs is important. The local employers are used to hiring international students and familiar with their visa sponsorship requirements."

This advice made sense to me. Why would one study industrial engineering in rural Tennessee when the entire industry was in Detroit? The not-so-attractive number five on my list, Eastern Michigan University was now, I realized, the better option. I happily accepted their offer and returned paperwork through someone traveling to the U.S., begging them to mail it as soon as they arrived.

When we applied for the U.S. student visa in Madras, Sarat's application was rejected while mine was approved. During that year of preparing, Sarat and I had become good friends. It was a sad moment for both of us. In fact, it was a worse disappointment for Sarat's father, who dreamt of Sarat studying and settling in the U.S. He even accompanied Sarat to Madras to support him, while I had to go alone.

Dejected, Sarat decided to seek employment in India after graduation, and my hunt for money began. Eastern Michigan University operated in a quarter system, so that annual costs would be $12,000 in tuition and $10,000 in living expenses. That would total $44,000 for the two-year program. International students were only allowed to work on campus for limited hours. Even if I got a part-time job to help cover my living costs, I still needed $5,000 for just the first term fees and travel costs. Whatever else we could get together would go toward living expenses, books, clothing, and incidentals.

Clearly, we couldn't afford much, but the idea was to take the minimum amount needed for the first term, then figure it out as I went along, semester-by-semester. Whatever it took to survive there, I would work as hard as needed while studying. I started trying to raise the $5,000 I needed. We had a few wealthy relatives on my mother's side of the family. My first thought was to hit them up for $500 apiece. All I needed was ten generous benefactors to get $5,000. My mother wanted to show off her son, but she wouldn't entertain the idea of asking ten relatives for money. She was too proud. Nevertheless, we went on a four-day road trip to her relatives in other nearby villages.

Invariably at every home, as we sat down for lunch, dinner, or afternoon tea, the question of the high cost of studying abroad came up, I would then take the opportunity and explain that, if possible, I could use assistance. I would never directly ask for the whole $500, even from those that wouldn't have minded giving it to me. Everyone we visited gave me a little for my expenses. By the end of the trip, it added up to Rs.20,000, about $700. I was pleased, but I still needed another $4,300.

I decided the best thing to do was ask my wealthiest relatives, Indra Babai, for a small loan of Rs.100,000, about $3,000. He was one of the most successful entrepreneurs in the district. His son lived in the U.S. Indra Babai had been friends with my father and had great regard for him. His wife was my mother's cousin. He would help for sure; I persuaded her to contact him. He was pleased at her request but told her that I had to meet with him since I required the loan. I had always stopped by Indra Babai's home whenever I went to the village, but this time I was reluctant to step into their house. Asking for money felt shameful.

I had been summoned, so I dragged myself there to plead my case. When he saw me, he pulled me close to him and held my hand with both his hands, congratulating me. "I am delighted for your future. Your father always had big dreams for you. Your mother struggled a lot since he passed. It's lucky you are getting this opportunity to go to America; make the most of it and take care of your family. I watched you grow over the years, and I want you to know that I believe in you. I am more than happy to help you realize your dreams."

He then added, "But I am not doing this for your mother or your deceased father. I am doing it for you. I sensed your hesitation in approaching me for money. Don't be bashful in life, it is important to boldly seek help when needed. That is why I asked to see you."

Tears welled in my eyes listening to him and his warmth for me and my family. Including the $700 from the field trip and the $3,000 Indra Babai agreed to loan, I was still $1,300 short, which my mother offered to cover somehow. There was no way that I could earn the money, on an engineer's starting salary of $100/month. There were only a few weeks left before I was to leave.

Luckily the government had recently started a study abroad loan program offering interest free loans repayable within three years after the completion of the degree, but they needed introductions and personal guaranty signatures from two adults with good financial standing. The bank approved the application for the $3,300 after my cousin Chinni Akka's husband, and Vasu Babai, whom I had been pleading with for months, signed on as guarantors.

I now had $7,000 available, more than my $5,000 target. We set the travel dates, bought my plane tickets, a few new clothes, and supplies that we imagined I would need, including a small battery-operated alarm clock. I decided to take only what was needed for my first term fees and a little extra to get started, leaving the excess funds with Chinni Akka's husband for safekeeping; I would ask him to send it when needed. The understanding was if I didn't need that amount, he would put it to use and repay the loan in full when it came due.

As a final farewell trip before the journey, I went back to our village home and was welcomed by extended family and village elders. It was a big deal that one of their own was striking out for America. It seemed most of the village wanted to meet me, inviting me to stop by their homes before I left.

I had avoided the family's farm since my father's death. I went there one final time on the last day in the village and buried the Rs 100 note he had given me in the spot where he was cremated. I'd suppressed many memories since his death, but this was my way of honoring him and reconciling the last ten years. I realized that had my father not set me a path that ended up in Hyderabad, prioritizing my education, I may have never found myself in this situation.

All misgivings aside I was grateful. On the last day of my trip, I was introduced to a young man, Ajay, who'd just returned from the U.S. for summer break. We soon realized he was attending the same university in Michigan. He was two years ahead of me and gave me some advice about campus life, promising to show me around. He stayed the entire summer in India. It was a stroke of luck to find someone else going to the same university.

Meena's mother decided the time was right to tell her husband about Meena and me. She invited me to Hyderabad to meet him at their home. It was an uneventful, pleasant meeting. I told him that I met Meena at college, and that we liked each other. I explained that I was going to the U.S. for graduate school and that she could join me after her graduation, and we would come back to India and marry after we got jobs. We wanted his blessing before I left for the U.S.

He congratulated me and wished me well without asking much of anything else. He seemed satisfied with the situation. I could tell he liked me, he joked with me and shook my hand. Having watched many Bollywood movies that depicted such meetings ending disastrously, I was prepared for the worst. But he made me feel welcome. Later, Meena told me her mother had briefed him on the entire situation, speaking very positively about me, and convincing him about the plan. It turned out that was the reason for his quick consent. What a great woman!

Since the day Meena's mother had come to meet me, we developed a good relationship, not the typical son-in-law/mother-in-law dynamic. Over time, she came to see me as the son she never had and confided in me at times, seeking my input on important issues. She appreciated my help with her youngest brother's family relocation to the U.S., and in ensuring a good marriage for her second daughter. Her warmth and respect towards me for everything I wanted to do for my family was clear from her bond with my mother and sisters. It was easy for me to feel attached to my mother-in-law, with her soft demeanor, welcoming smile, and easy-going attitude.

Some in my family worried that if I couldn't find good employment given all the visa-related restrictions, and I might end up like the poor students working demeaning jobs at gas stations, scrubbing toilets, flipping burgers at fast food chains. Given the cheap workforce in India, such physical work was given little dignity and was often ridiculed. Several of my cousins got discouraged from pursuing their dreams for fear of failure or such mockery. "Why do you want to go all the way to the U.S. and wipe their toilets, while we can afford to hire many to clean ours here?"

Other people said, "Everyone that has left for the U.S. before you never came back. we know you are going for good."

I'd rejected such statements. Distance does have a way of loosening the bonds of relationships. But it seemed rude and selfish for people to leave their homes and their loved ones to fly away great distances like that and never return.

"I am not like that. I will not do that," I told everyone. "My goal is to complete my studies, find a job, earn, and save to bring home Rs 1 crore, so I can care for my family the way I want. I am not going to stay in the U.S. I promise." That was it, my audacious goal: the amount of money that qualified someone as a millionaire in Indian rupees was only $300,000, Rs 1 crore!

On the big day of my departure, I had two cheap suitcases stuffed and almost bursting. We got to Hyderabad airport three hours early, over sixty people came to see me off including family, friends, and Meena. I was touched by the turnout.

My mother and father each had six siblings, out of all of them and my twenty-eight cousins, I was the first to go to the U.S. It was a big deal. They were all eager to show their support and send me off with their best wishes. Krishna uncle was proud, though disappointed that his dream for me to join the Indian Administrative Services would go unfulfilled. Everyone praised him for all his work putting me on this path.

Raja Babai, who up until then wanted me to stay in India, bought me a mini padlock as a reminder to return with my $300,000. Memories of my father still seemed fresh in everyone's minds, even ten years after he had passed away. He was a well-loved person within the family, and all that love towards him and sympathy for my mother poured in as goodwill towards me. I went from person to person with tears in my eyes, thanking them for their support.

India, with its traditions around the importance of family and friends, has a way of pulling on you. There are Indian traditions that remain with me, deep in my mind, the importance of family being the foremost. It was hard to fly away from my home, my family. It feels like your body is leaving while your soul remains behind, like you are a heartless soul distancing yourself from all that love, you are a little lost getting further and further away from all that warmth. It feels like a part of you is buried deep in that soil.

With $4,000 tucked away, my visa and passport in hand, I boarded the flight in search of my destiny, leaving my entire life behind, the girl of my dreams, my mother, my two sisters, and my entire extended family that I so longed for all my life and never wanted to leave. I tried my best to remember it was all in the name of love.

# 6

## The Beginnings of an Alien Life

**LEAP OF FAITH**
**SUMMER 1993**

A T THE AGE OF TWENTY-ONE, I landed in Detroit to pursue my two year Industrial Technology Master's degree. My journey from Hyderabad was my first time in an airplane, but it wasn't that impressive. The food was unpalatable, and the orange drink reeked of chemicals that made me gag, not like the flavorful dishes and the sweetness of the freshly squeezed juices back home.

I was fearful of loneliness living somewhere I didn't know anyone, and still haunted by dreadful memories of my childhood. At the beginning of my life in the U.S. I quietly wept most of the time, missing everyone. The most difficult thing was parting from Meena. This was closely followed by the pressure of getting together the customary dowry that was needed for my sisters when they got married, and the expected wedding expenses. Had my father been alive, the pressure of providing for these marriages would have been on his shoulders. But, given the situation, it came down to my mother and me. I would have to start earning money quickly.

Unlike most international students who are eager to experience the American way of life, I was less excited about my new life than I was worried about my way forward. Usually, foreign students arrive only a day or two before the term begins, to maximize the time back home while minimizing costs. I arrived from India almost thirty days before classes started, hoping to immediately find work, not only to survive but also to get money for next term's tuition. Even though I was in college, for me, there would be little time for fun.

The first thing to hit me as I ventured out to explore the campus was its vastness. Having been a neat freak all my life everything looked new, clean, and orderly and the freshness of the air impressed me—it was so different from India. When I got there the campus was mostly empty classrooms and offices. I was fascinated by the beautiful structures, the oversized lecture halls, the computers everywhere, the open spaces, the wide roads, and the lush greenery. The huge stadiums, particularly the student center and the gymnasium, impressed me the most.

By contrast, my engineering college in India, although located on a large campus of forty acres, lacked suitable buildings and facilities. Even the computer lab had only twenty machines. The entire city of Vijayawada, where my college was located, did not have one such impressive stadium or gymnasium.

My dorm room, the food, even the milk—everything was different. I noticed students drinking water from the household taps, something we would never do in India where we had to boil or filter tap water before drinking it. The sights and smells around the residence halls were almost otherworldly to me, and it was quiet everywhere. In India, there was always a buzz, from the street hawkers, the motorcycles, the whirring auto-rickshaws, people chatting along the road, the aroma from a neighbor's kitchen; all the liveliness from home was missing. There was an eerie quietness about everything around that made me hesitate even to speak.

Whenever I met anyone, I inquired about job openings. On my second day there, I got a lead. Someone failed to show up at the kitchen at one of the dorms. It didn't take much to get the job: washing dishes in the back room, serving food behind the counters, refilling the empty trays for $4.25/hr. I wasn't going to make a million dollars right away, but I was already better off than I was less than a week before. Working at this campus job allowed me to earn $340 a month. I was relieved. Now, I knew I could make it.

After asking around about ways to get a better job I learned I needed a resume, something I had never even heard of before. In India, we called them biodata, which was similar but different. Highlighting every bit of my experience with computers, engineering, procuring, marketing, leadership, even listing my driving skills, I printed my first resume on the first Macintosh I ever touched. Fifty copies in hand, I started knocking on doors.

In addition to learning the nuances about resumes and the drinkable water, I also learned quickly about American etiquette. When I visited a Key Bank to open an account, I casually ignored the line of about five or six people, and confidently walked to the front of the counter, totally oblivious to everyone around me, asserting my need for immediate service. When others had complained about cutting a line back home, it felt heroic. You were doing what was needed to get ahead, being smart, and avoided getting lost in the crowd. In India, if you are hesitant you are bound to be left behind. Anyone that wants to get anywhere in life learns to hustle. But in America, this behavior, I learned, wasn't heroic, it was just rude.

Back home you were considered weak for being civil with the justification that everyone else does it too. As I cut in front an older lady tapped me on my shoulder with a big smile and calmly gestured toward the end of the line, without even saying a word. I started seeing the orderliness of everything around me over the next few weeks.

The level of consumerism in the U.S. struck me the most and confused me. There was an abundance of choices for everything. Back in India during the Eighties, there were three or four brands of cars with one or two models, and a few brands of toothpaste. Here just walking through a grocery or department store aisle was an experience in learning how to filter choices and deciphering the marketing clutter.

With my generally liberal approach to money until then, everything around me was tempting, all the shoes, clothes even cars. However, after being here a bit, something changed. I am not sure if it was the uncertainty of my current situation or the certainty of difficult things coming soon. But I started getting very serious about not spending any money I didn't have to. No one said it was required, it just happened.

Within the first four weeks I became friends with a few other senior students from India and decided to share a two bedroom off campus apartment with three others. It allowed me to save considerably on boarding costs, and I could cover the expenses from my campus job earnings. But I worried about the cost of future tuition fees. The only way to cover these costs was to find a paid Graduate Assistant post. GA's received a full tuition waiver, plus a monthly stipend. However, such positions were rare and highly sought after; every competent graduate student wanted one, and competition was tough. The second week after classes began, I bumped into Ajay. Coming across a person that shares the same roots in an unfamiliar environment makes one's heart jump with joy.

Ajay was a Graduate Assistant and only had one course left before graduating. He was on his way to his GA job. We spoke for a few minutes, and I brought him up to speed on my activities over the past few weeks in my relentless quest for a GA role. He promised to catch up after jotting down my contact details. Two days later, Ajay called me. He'd received a job offer from an IT firm in California, and his professor tasked him with finding his GA replacement. Given the short notice, they were in a rush to fill the role as they had immediate teaching needs to support.

I asked to interview for the position, and he set it up for the following Monday. My interviews with two professors were successful, and by that Wednesday afternoon, I was hired as their next Graduate Assistant. Combined with the tuition waiver, it was like getting paid $18,000 a year.

Mother had relocated back to our village Vundrajavaram around that time. Calling her was complicated. First, it was expensive, costing $2 per minute. We could not talk long, and by the time the pleasantries were exchanged it would be time to hang up. And she did not have a home phone. The only way to reach her was to call the nearby clothing store. Karthi Bava, Krishna uncle's eldest son, worked at the telephones department in India. Taking advantage of the free calls from the government phone lines, he would call me on occasion and keep my mother abreast of my progress.

She was delighted to hear the GA news and told me she never doubted my abilities. Since my GA role was awarded just a few days after classes started, my first term fees were covered by the university in full. Within a few weeks the entire tuition I'd paid earlier was refunded. Encouraged by how I was able to find my way around my campus, I called my friend Sarat's father in India, inquiring about Sarat's whereabouts and giving him an update about my progress. Sarat had relocated to Bangalore by then and started working at a small firm. I pleaded with his father to call him in and to apply a second time right away.

Honestly, I was desperate to have him join me in the U.S. Luckily for Sarat, his father convinced him to quickly give it another try. Within a couple of weeks, I received the good news that Sarat had secured his visa and that he would enroll at a university in Alabama after Christmas.

Not only was I settling in at my university but soon I would have my old friend around as well. I was very relieved and unbelievably happy because I thought I would not feel so alone. By Thanksgiving, I had returned the $3,000 Indra Babai loaned to me only four months after receiving it. I was now debt-free, pursuing an independently funded education, earning $650 monthly.

That first Christmas in the U.S., seeing snow and throwing snowballs for the first time in my life, was magical. Watching people everywhere enjoying their snowmobiles, cross-country skiing, skating on the frozen lakes, skiing in the mountains, I fancied participating in all that, but couldn't justify the expense. But playing with the snow was free, so I did that.

At times, in our apartment, my roommates and I boarded students who came to the Detroit area after finishing their master's degrees. They came searching for jobs in the auto capital of the world. It's tough to turn away a fellow student in need. Whenever we got a request for temporary housing, I felt fortunate having ended up there. There was no dearth of company over the weekends.

All that activity still couldn't help me overcome the lonely, homesick feelings when school or work activities didn't keep me occupied. Missing everyone back home, particularly Meena, made me impatient and petulant at times. I would occasionally snap at friends or get moody, not do my usual weekend activities preferring to be left alone with my thoughts. It brought back memories of my lonely childhood at Krishna uncle's home, in Hyderabad. It seems feeling lonely has little to do with physically being alone.

Another aspect of my life in the U.S. that interestingly established my own identity and set me apart like many other immigrants was my Indian name. While often well meaning, many folks have a hard time at first pronouncing an Indian name. In my case I always took it as an opportunity to interact positively with someone. It would usually start with someone giving it a shot and stumble a bit. "Go ahead and say it," I'd encourage them.

"No, I can't. I am afraid, I'd butcher it," they'd shyly refuse.

"Say it just the way it reads ... It's okay, you won't hurt my feelings ... Say it like a Tree with an S." That always seemed to help put people at ease.

Even at school, if someone called and asked, "May I speak with, er, er, er ..." trying to pronounce it letter by letter or one syllable at a time, our department administrator would simply transfer them to me, assuming it must be for me. Someone once even asked if my name was Italian! Seeing how difficult it was, I considered trying to avoid the problem, as other Asians had by switching to a more American name. Some changed their names to that of Hollywood stars. In different places I used different names, switching between Harry and James. Each time it felt rather silly and uncomfortable responding, as though I was playing some role in a play; the only difference is I could be stuck with it for life. Finally, I decided simply responding to a butchered version of my given name was the least torturous for me and easier for everyone else. After all, a given name carries meaning, especially because Indian parents go to so much effort to pick them.

Back home, everyone got stacks of letters from me. I wrote to everyone: my cousins, friends, sisters, and especially my mother and Meena. Sunday was my letter writing day. It was during those days I got closer to Meena's sister Radha, when she started writing to me about her life in Hyderabad. It took about seven to ten days for a letter to travel each way. I anxiously waited for responses to my letters. Sometimes multiple letters would arrive back-to-back, weeks later. But given the high cost of phone calls, there was no other option.

Meena was finishing her final year of engineering degree. She also had been admitted to a university in Detroit. Her path was relatively more straightforward than mine had been, thanks to my "expert" guidance on the ins and outs of graduate school and being a foreign student. We were both dreaming about meeting in the U.S. in a few months, and then my loneliness would finally be over.

.       .       .

## PLANS?
## WINTER 1994

By January, I had passed the additional certification exams that demonstrated my engineering aptitude, helping to give me an edge in employment. I had saved $250 a month from my GA earnings. I started sending little amounts of money and gifts back to India. I arranged for a phone at our village home and got my mother's bedroom in India set up with an AC unit, replaced her old refrigerator and TV. My younger sister, Sasi enrolled in a local MBA program. Wanting to ease the strain on my mother, I sent the money for the fees. Deepa did not want to pursue higher education after completing her business degree. She was staying with my mother.

Although both my sisters were educated, they weren't the career-minded women that would venture out seeking a professional life. This was often the case in families like ours. Other than one or two career-oriented female cousins, the option of pursuing professional employment wasn't generally up for discussion. Most education for women was meant to enrich family lives and come in handy when raising children. An arranged marriage after completing education was the logical step where society is not geared for women to work professionally outside the home. This is disappointing for a country that had a woman head of government long before many western countries, including the U.S.

Twenty-two or twenty-three was considered the right age for middle-class Indian girls to marry. Later than that might create rumors about their attractiveness or their prospects, especially in fatherless families, except if they were open about their attitudes about arranged marriages or were pursuing post graduate education.

Deepa was almost twenty-one years old. We could not delay the marriage process. I often wished my sisters were younger by a few more years, because we would have had more time to organize and plan everything as well as possible. But instead, I was racing against time.

Eager to earn some quick money for Deepa's wedding, I considered taking a break from my studies to work and make cash off the books. A few of the students had acquired summer jobs in Florida or Connecticut through their social networks. It was essentially a rite of passage for the poor students. It wasn't unusual for the most hardworking to come back with $10,000 in cash stuffed into hidden pockets of their duffle bags. An acquaintance had a lead on a job as a cab driver in Chicago. I could work a few months and return to campus and continue with school. I must admit the idea of being a cab driver was intriguing.

Many people who had known me since my childhood had always wondered if I would be able to handle grueling long hours working flipping greasy burgers, serving burnt coffee, stacking grocery shelves, or working at dreary gas stations as some other Indian immigrants did. The significant difference for me was my ability and willingness to drive for hours. Most Indian students arriving in the U.S. only learned to drive in some parking lot once they got here, therefore generally had poor driving skills, at least initially.

My uncle Vasu Babai had owned a car, which we fondly referred to by its license number, "8316", a ramshackle assemblage of a vehicle that broke down at every opportunity. Due to lack of funds Vasu Babai kept it operational rather than splurging on a new car. Keeping it going was both an art and a science. As far as the family was concerned keeping it moving was on par with being a skilled pilot. I learned to drive at seventeen; switch out flat tires, dead batteries, carburetors; and change leaky oil filters. We drove over four-foot-high hay piles that were strewn on roads in rural India, through mud puddles, bumpy paddy fields, crawled across three-foot deep ditches. We drove around with the muffler tied together with jute rope, used a flashlight as a headlight, and routinely transported a pack of kids to the movies. That beautiful hunk of junk made a driver out of me.

If there was one thing I could do with the utmost confidence, it was drive. So being offered this cabbie opportunity seemed like a sign. I would arrive in April in Chicago after finishing my winter session. I made arrangements to share an apartment for four months with other cab drivers. I dreamed of heading back to campus with loads of cash.

However, before I could start, my housemate and good friend, Naren, pulled me aside. He said he was vaguely aware of some family obligations back home but told me I was thinking too short-term and not making a wise choice. "Despite everything, I would still advise you against it. To fulfill some portion of your commitments, if $20,000 or so is what you may need, you should simply get a few low-interest credit cards, cash them out and send money home, rather than take a job as a cab driver in Chicago. It's a slippery slope that many get sucked into getting used to the easy cash income, some even quit university. That is not the future you should step into ... under any circumstances." Hard to hear but true nonetheless, in the end I was grateful for this bit of advice.

Naren had been making the summer trips to Connecticut, working at a donut store. He did not have a GA to cover his tuition and had to pay for college. He reminded me of the actual situation I was facing and not be so small in my outlook or end goal. "Why do you want to waste your time chasing quick money driving cabs? Instead, you should focus on getting your degree as quickly as possible and finding a full-time job." He was absolutely right, and I started to think of ways to land a summer internship or job as soon as possible.

Shortly thereafter, I saw a flyer for an engineering conference. It cost $1500 for professionals, but only $50 for students. I figured many corporate managers would attend such a conference and it would be a good opportunity to network. After the conference I started making inquiries into job prospects at some of the companies. On the second day, the owner of a small automation company returned one of the many calls I had made. He invited me to meet him in person two days later and while he did not need an intern, he liked my enthusiasm and promised to get back to me.

That same evening, another company also called. He said they had their trainees, but since my request was for an unpaid internship, I got an in-person interview. The following day after the interview I was offered an apprenticeship, but they made it a paid assignment. Their factory worked in two shifts, the engineering team worked the first, from 7 am to 3:30 pm. A couple of days later, the automation company owner also called me back as promised; he had dreamt up a pet project he had been putting off that badly needed some attention and wanted me to do it. I thanked him for the offer and explained about my new internship starting soon. But I offered to work from 4 pm to 10 pm, he went for it, and I got thirty hours a week at the second company. I was in mild shock at these two successes in a row.

Just a few weeks before, I'd been preparing to be a cab driver, now I had two jobs doing what I was here to do. The long hours for the two jobs did not bother me, and the opportunity to make this money for my sister was rewarding and satisfying. The problem was transportation. My plan was to take the public bus, but there was no way to get there quickly enough. I had to get a car. I only had $1000 in my savings account, so a beat-up, rusty car would be my only option.

My roommate and closest friend, Seenu, already owned one such clunker, a well-worn black Nissan Maxima from the early 80s. Nevertheless, I requested Seenu's permission to drive this monster, since the car was not used much on weekdays. He agreed that I would use it for my internship runs, and he would use it over the weekend. A perfect arrangement. I would of course keep it filled up with gas and pay for repairs to keep it running.

The following few months flew by quickly, with me seeing little sunlight on those pleasantly cool spring and sunny summer days. I was able to call home more often because the new long-distance cards cost only eight cents per minute, a far cry from the $2 until then. Our letter writing slowly lost out to cheap telecommunications. We were free to make as many calls as we wanted, talk all we wanted—within our budgets. Everything was going well until the middle of the summer of 1994, when Meena's visa application was denied—possibly crushing her dreams of a U.S. education and us being together. Our plans, our hopes imploded.

# 7

## Trying to Tie It All Up

**RUSH TO SETTLE**
**SUMMER 1994**

WHEN MEENA WAS DENIED a student visa a second time, I wanted to circumvent the visa issues and help pursue her studies as planned; we thought of me going back to India immediately to get married. But this would not go over well back home.

I still floated the idea of marrying first with my mother, who promptly shot it down, as expected. "Young men in our families do not get married without arranging their sisters' marriages first. I understand your predicament, but what is the rush for her to join you there? You don't even have a proper job yet. It is unfortunate, but Meena can stay here. Let us seek alliances for Deepa. You must wait at least until her wedding. There is no other way."

My best argument with my mother was that my student visa would expire potentially leaving me with insufficient time to find a good job. But she would have none of it. These sort of practical logistical hassles that could make or break our future didn't seem to register with her, only the customs and traditions. Since I had two younger sisters who were not married, I had to wait until they got married first.

Disheartened, I asked my mother to rush the search for a suitable groom for Deepa. Had I gone against her wishes and only thought of Meena and my interests, it would be scandalous to have gone against the family. Growing up, one of the core messages I heard consistently from everyone around me, "Make your family proud of you, do not do anything that would disgrace your family name." Perhaps this has been deeply ingrained in my psyche and that's why I could not muster the courage to override my mother's ruling on such an important matter. I did not want to do anything to tarnish the family name any more than what had already been done by my father.

Due to these setbacks Meena had begun to slip into a mildly depressive state. We were both emotionally overwhelmed for several months. A long-distance relationship maintained by occasional phone calls and letters was very difficult and kept me on edge, increasing my mood swings and loneliness to the point where my friends worried about me. Meena and I were desperate to see each other. I decided the best thing was to pursue a full-time job right away and get an employment visa. Expediting all the plans we had in mind after Meena joined me would allow me to support Meena and improve the chances of changing my mother's opinion of our marriage. I updated my resume and started scouring the help wanted ads, trying to leverage my recent work experience.

I was invited to interview for an engineer's job with an automotive parts supplier. When I returned to my apartment after the interview, I was met by the blinking light of a voice message. I got the job! The next week, I received a formal offer of full-time employment as an engineer, with health insurance and other benefits, for $40,000 a year. The company wanted me to begin right away and offered to sponsor my visa. My start date was two weeks away, but back home, Meena's mental state had worsened.

After graduating from engineering college, she had moved back to her parents' home and that return wasn't as easy as it seemed to be. Meena had become accustomed to being on her own over the prior four years other than holidays. Adjusting to life at home with her sister and parents made her feel as though she was an outsider and not in her own home. Added to this, other than her parents and her sister, none of her relatives knew about us. But I was sure that the marriage of a twenty-one-year-old girl to an eligible graduate engineer would be regarded as worthy match by most Indian relatives.

Since no one knew about us, unbeknownst to Meena or her parents, her extended family had started scouring their networks, for suitable grooms entirely on their own. Slowly a litany of candidates was being proposed. The polite deflections of her parents were ignored, as they had to reject each proposal individually. It got to the point where without their knowledge, one enthusiastic relative arranged a formal meet and greet session with a groom recently returned from the U.S.—who waited for her at their home.

Meena had to go through with the charade, only to eventually reject the match citing some farcical reason. I sort of pity the poor guy's loss, but it was without question my gain. Her relatives weren't thrilled, but they accepted it, and kept searching. Overcome with the stresses of getting her visa rejected and the adjustment to moving back home after college, and all these marriage-related pressures from her relatives, she joined a meditation group and adopted a philosophical view of life. Everyone was worried about her, and I spent countless hours on the phone talking with her about what was going on, trying to be supportive and lift her spirits.

Despite those struggles, based on the missteps that pushed her family apart in the coming years, Meena later felt the visa being rejected at least gave her the opportunity to spend another year with her mother, for which she was grateful. It was the longest stretch of time she spent with her family since high school.

After several difficult years of losing money, the automotive parts firm that hired me had decided to try to restructure and rebuild, and that's where I fit in. They hired me as a junior and another engineer as the senior manager to run the department and to start on the same day. Unfortunately, the other new hire did not show up, instantly making me the new one-person engineering department. By the third month, I could sort of see that it was a sinking ship, and I could not risk my visa by getting sponsored by them. If the company went down while my paperwork was in process, I would be ineligible to remain in the U.S. and subject to major visa hassles. My entire future would be at stake.

Within a month, however, I was able to get another job with a much larger auto parts supplier that was in the process of being acquired by a German manufacturer. Meena got a job at an architectural firm in Hyderabad. Thankfully, it was a distraction from the unhealthy thoughts that had been engulfing her. She had developed a new circle of friends who had professional jobs and began spending time with them, visiting cafes, movies, shows, usual twenty-one-year-old activities.

I completed my master's degree with honors and was on the Dean's list. Towards the end of that summer, my job required me to visit China and India. By then I hadn't seen Meena and my family in almost two years! I was ready to visit home. I was excited that my first trip back to India would be a business trip, a perfect reflection of my early success in the U.S.

I finally started feeling comfortable with the way my life unfolded in the U.S. In addition to Sarat, a few other close friends of ours from our engineering college, and a couple of other cousins also arrived in the U.S. to go to graduate school. We started meeting up. I managed to help a few of them with the admissions process and was also able to help with their tuition and expenses, lending them the money they needed to get started, saving them the hassle of borrowing from someone in India like I had to.

The past two years seemed like a decade of activity. If I could get my family settled it seemed that I fulfill my biggest responsibility. I hoped it would all come together during my visit to India. Deepa's marriage was to be arranged, somehow, by December 1995. No suitable groom had been found in over a year and a half of "intensive search." Meena was desperately awaiting my return; she was already admitted to my university for the following year. My mother and sisters were anxious to have me come back. Because I had done well at my job over the past year I had fewer financial constraints, and I was eager to see everyone.

· · ·

## IDEAL ARRANGEMENTS
## SUMMER 1995

The plan, while straight forward was not simple: I was to find a husband for Deepa, get married myself, and bring Meena back to the U.S.—all in an ungodly short time. Meena's parents and my family agreed to a wedding date set for early December. My mother wanted me to wait until Deepa's match was at least arranged, but she understood the predicament Meena's parents were in as well, so we went ahead. Nearly everything was in place for two weddings back-to-back.

A perfect plan, the only problem was that one groom was missing. If my intent were simply to get Deepa married off quickly to the first prospect I came across, it would have been quick, but it wasn't. My sisters were sensible, lively souls; and pleasant, caring girls with their own talents. Growing up in my mother's care, they knew how to share their love and affection with others. They were raised a little sheltered, which required they be married to the right man. Based on my understanding of their aspirations and desires, I was clear on what sort of a person would suit their needs and my concerns.

My family looked for a groom from a respectable family with a traditional lineage and background like ours, but with better finances; whereas I was seeking a groom who had demonstrated a family-oriented nature with the potential to be a self-made person with good job and education qualifications. Having experienced what was available in the U.S., I wanted to find someone capable of emigrating, not just someone rooted in their family's past glory. There was a serious mismatch in what I wanted of the grooms and those being advanced by my relatives. I kept obstinately rejecting multiple prospects as a result.

Traditional middle-class Indian "arranged marriages" were uniquely prejudiced affairs. They revolved around the perceived merits of the family, lineage, finances, social stature, and qualifications. It went beyond the happiness or character of the people involved. The one key element of the Indian arranged marriage was the elders' making choices for their grown-up kids. It wasn't just the parents; it was uncles, aunts, grandparents, siblings, and the entire extended family enthusiastically playing matchmaker.

In an ideal situation elders would draw from their myriad life experiences and knowledge of their child's desires and wants. The elders guided the child on choices to serve their future needs, hoping for a good marriage. All the boxes that one checked on some matchmaking website to narrow down their choices, the family filled in the boxes knowing what may be best. It was like a human version of match.com.

Of course, the bride and the groom had the final say, having to decide based on the one or two opportunities they got to meet, or a few months of contact during more modern times. Adults found a suitable match, they were given opportunities to talk and engage with each other, and a decision was made. The choice rested on the family as much as the bride and groom. The cultural notion was that when one marries into a family, one also marries the entire family, not just the individual.

Families rooted in their traditional worlds had reputations going back generations, which by and large determined their station in society. If that position was not supported by the current generation's actions or financial success, their social stature diminished. Conversely, if someone managed to improve their reputation or economic position in one generation, their social standing got bumped up. The sibling, parental, and extended family's histories, their influence within the community, their financial stability, everything was carefully reviewed with microscopic precision. "You must look into the past seven generations and study their values before allying with a family," was a saying I often heard in India.

While marriages like these were handled as a family business deal hinging on those multiple factors, most needed to be checked off as prerequisites to a successful union. Whether they led to lasting happiness or not was debatable. The reality was many times these arranged marriages led to poor matches and unsuccessful marriages due to misplaced priorities, character, or personality differences. Check the wrong box, and one ends up with the wrong results.

Indian society has a pragmatic view of a marital relationship. They believe compromise and an ability to adapt was the most important thing to keep a marriage together. Of course, the need for love in that marriage is not discounted or ignored. The underlying assumption was the marrying couple would come to love and care for each other after their union.

They would remain committed to it, having been raised to respect the institution of marriage. Their family could offer guidance and counseling to help them one step at a time. It worked for people who grew up within that environment, particularly those conditioned to accept the custom, and understand and respect the arrangements. An entire social ecosystem was built on this most important of social relationships.

The ideal arranged marriage has the right amount of give and take between both sides. Both families got something they wanted, something they feel enhanced their life. It was the way of arranged marriages. Owing to our financial hardships, no family with a strong reputation or financial stability would consider us. By default, anyone suggested to us had weak finances that others felt would suit our station, village folk with some inheritance who would be content to lead a decent life in the countryside were seen as the target demographic.

Influenced by Rao Tatha and others with well-intentioned but traditional mindsets, my mother was considering a few such prospects, willing to get her eldest daughter married as quickly as possible. She was painfully aware of our limitations and, as a result, had a limited view of the possibilities. But at the same time, she had a layer of wishful thinking, hoping for something better for her daughter. Deepa would consent to anyone approved by my mother and me.

I started being responsible for the family affairs, as though I was the head of the family, because their approach to the whole marriage concerned me. Given the intricate hierarchical structures of Indian families, I was seen as arrogant with my increasingly strident views from America, defying the elders and their judgement. That's when I deliberately leaned on my reputation and put my foot down. Perhaps, my upbringing with Krishna uncle came in handy.

Indian society has a way of serving as an intricately complex canvas for the active mind and the challenge seeking soul. I knew that within the same stratum, both sides looked for the best prospect they could land within a narrower socio-financial "bracket." Not the bracket they wishfully fancied in a silly boastful way, or the bracket in their egoistic mind, but the bracket others in their social circle saw them fitting into, forced them into, mostly based on their family lineage, wealth, income prospects and such. The key to success and satisfaction is understanding which socio-economic bracket each family belongs to with complete honesty, humility, clarity. One rarely had the chance to jump brackets at the time of the marriage unless there were extenuating circumstances, such as a penniless bride vaguely resembling a movie star or a model of some sort that the wealthy groom drools over or an impoverished groom with such extraordinary skills as a qualified doctor or an engineer with exceptional credentials. Rarely, it included a wealthy Samaritan seeking a thoughtful alliance for their offspring with one from a simple family of little means but high character. All the goodwill in the world is necessary to land a better alliance within your bracket.

To me, the groom's family history was vital, but not at the groom's expense. I believed a worthy person could jump any number of brackets from their own actions. An irresponsible person would bring themselves and their family down over time, thereby getting shunned and moving down multiple brackets unceremoniously. It is entirely on the individual, their ambition, focus, talent, opportunity, and hard work where they could end up. I cautioned my mother against prioritizing lineage, pressing her to find the person with the best chance of getting ahead now while loving and caring for Deepa. For me, that was the only acceptable way forward, the only way to jump the bracket in due course, to find the right person with the best traits, not the one with the best past lineage.

In the end we had to jump brackets creatively to find suitable husbands for both my sisters. I couldn't entirely rely on the folks back home to do that, with their old notions of success, bound by their own limitations. My sisters had to be well matched and provided for. I was single-mindedly focused on that. Typical for families those days, the bulk of the assets went to the sons. Families gave whatever dowry they could reasonably get away with to the girls at the time of the marriage. When looked at as a percentage of assets available, even the largest dowries given were still quite small compared to the family's net worth, unless the family had little to begin with.

My mother loved her girls and did everything she could for them, but at the end of the day, she was partial towards me, her only son. "The girls take the assets and leave home, usually selling the land given to them at some point later. Then it isn't in the family anymore. The boys carry the family lineage and should be the heirs to the bulk of the assets," my mother told me. This was in line with the common thinking, aided by the tradition that the sons were expected to care for the family members when they are older and therefore needed the bulk of the assets.

"The girls might be supported later if required, as and when you achieve further success and stability in your own life," she added. I had no intention of living in the village and was confident I would be fine on my own without inheriting the land; after all my family gave me a great educational foundation. If I couldn't do something for my sisters at that time, given our limited assets, something would have to give and typically it would be my sisters that would suffer the most and I did not want that to happen.

Doing whatever it took to make my sisters self-sufficient at the time of their marriage made more sense to me than going with the conventional idea of helping them later. So, I advised her to split the assets between the girls at the time of their marriage, without saving anything for me or herself. I argued that my sisters needed it more right now.

"You do not have to keep a penny even for your own needs," I said, promising her that I would support her future needs and care for her well-being. When she pushed back, I told her, "That property will be insignificant to me when I've reached my full potential."

She admonished me for being foolhardy. But I was trying to make a point. I suggested that I could significantly increase the size of the dowry, that way Deepa could get a better match. And I'd been saving money for this reason. I said, "Finding good husbands needs us to put our best foot forward, as it's an irreversible process."

Unable to win the argument she nervously agreed to leave it to me.

As in many parts of the world, the bride's family was the primary bearer of the wedding expenses. In India it was meant to be a grand affair. Everyone tried to outdo each other, or at a minimum overextended themselves. While most nouveau riche and old monied folks spent hundreds of thousands or even millions, it's the pseudo rich who get themselves in real trouble by trying to "keep up with the Joneses," borrowing hundreds of thousands for the wedding alone. The feeling was that if the family did not go all out, even spending more than they had, they didn't do enough. While I was prepared to do what it took to ensure a successful marriage for my sisters, just like all those middle-class parents, I did not seek a penny from my in-laws for my wedding.

Marital stability is a significant contributor to the perceived success of the Indian diaspora within the western world. While their work ethic, pragmatism, reliance on education, and dual incomes drive much of their upward social mobility, the family structure is important as well.

Now that there was this upcoming business trip to India three months prior to my wedding, there was no more time to put off getting to work and making things happen.

.　　　.　　　.

### EARTHLY MATTERS
### SUMMER 1995

Before I could head to India as part of the normal rite of passage for immigrants, student, and professional aspirants, I had to jump through a few stupid bureaucratic hoops. The routine for folks needing the required visa was to fly into El Paso Texas, cross the border in a beat-up old van along with anyone else arriving around the same time. A sort of reverse cayote provided this service for a small fee for those with visa stamping needs, picked up everyone arriving within a specific time window.

He took us to a Red Roof Inn on the other side of the border, where the nastiest beds one could ever sleep in awaited us. I rested for the night the best I could, imagining bedbugs creeping up every crevice. I got picked up along with everyone else at 7 a.m. sharp. I stood in line with 50 to a 100 other people, waited my turn, pleaded my case to the consular officer, and prayed that I should be granted the visa. It was the required permit allowing me to travel outside the country.

Technically one couldn't reenter the U.S. if it was not approved. But since Mexico and Canada had travel arrangements with the U.S. not requiring one to produce a passport, one could reenter legally back then. Therefore, there was little risk, that's why it was essential to get this done here and not risk trying to have it stamped in China, my first travel destination, because if it got rejected for any reason I would risk getting stuck in China unable to reenter the U.S. and could then be forced to go back to India.

I got my visa approved. Not wanting to stay in Mexico any longer than necessary, I had the handler drop me off across the border on his evening run. My return flight to Michigan was not until the following day, so I decided to rent a car and drive up to the Carlsbad Caverns in New Mexico, about two hours away.

When I first arrived the wide-open roads in the U.S. made me feel like a kid in a candy store and driving too fast was my real vice, usually taking the speed limit signs as a mere "suggestion." I routinely got ticketed driving sixty in a twenty-five zone on neighborhood streets, ninety in fifty-five zones on highways.

On this occasion coming back from the caverns, I was driving through the scenic Guadalajara Mountain range, with the sun setting in front of me, the moon gently rising behind, visible in the rearview mirror, I had a clear view of the flat desert landscape. There were no trees, hills, or mountains to obscure the vistas and not another soul for miles, or so I thought. It was just bright orange skies, me, my car, and some music. That was the most picturesque scenery I'd ever seen.

I drove past a vehicle going the other direction, thirty minutes later, a white car parked along the side of the road with someone in a ten-gallon hat leaning on it appeared. Oblivious, I kept driving along, only to be pulled over by the same white car, a few minutes later—a policeman in an unmarked vehicle. After courteously asking for my ID and walking over to his car to check it out, he returned.

"Sir, do you have any idea why you were pulled over?"

"No, Officer, but I must have been driving over the speed limit."

"Yes, an officer that went the other way radioed us about your speed, and I have been waiting for you here for about fifteen minutes now," he said.

I apologized for my driving and just started running at the mouth, "This is the most picturesque place I've ever seen, Officer. I live in Michigan, but Texas has a special place in my imagination because of the Wild West movies." I explained I was from India, and I had never seen anything like it in real life. With the sun setting in front of me, the moon rising an almost complete view of the whole horizon, and the bright orange skies ... "I was just enjoying my drive and lost track of the speed. I am so sorry, Officer."

After staring at me for a long minute, he smiled, shook his head, and handed back my ID.

"Good day, Sir. Drive safely."

Thoroughly relieved, I thanked him profusely. Before shifting gears to take off, I turned around with a big smile.

"Officer, if you don't mind me asking, how fast was I going?"

"110 in a 45-mile zone, Sir," he said, smiling away and waving me off.

While this experience was positive (from my end especially) and almost touching, I had a very different encounter with the police that didn't go as well at first but became a lesson for everyone involved.

A year after this incident in Texas, driving through Birmingham, a small, wealthy, suburban town near Detroit, I got pulled over on a red-light violation. After checking my license, I was ordered to step out of the car, and I was arrested for driving with a suspended permit. Any explanations about possible errors were ignored and I was shoved onto the back of the police car.

Unlike back at home in India where I could have called someone who knew someone, who had a cousin, who could make a phone call and maneuver my way out of similar situations, there was no one for me to call in Michigan. I was driving with KP, my friend from India and Meena, who had both made it to the U.S. by then. They rushed to an ATM to get money for the fine and bail. Meanwhile, the police took mugshots and locked me up in a 4x10 cell with a cot and a steel toilet in the corner. It took the rest of the day to get the money together to get me out. I felt totally wronged, but there seemed to be little I could do at the time.

When later I was told there might be something I could do to make the court hear my case because the law said so—that I didn't have to know someone to pull strings—I was grateful that Michigan was in fact not India. After some time filing paperwork and counter claims and evidence that exonerated me (lengthy letters containing all the information necessary with ample proof the light was yellow and not red, that my license appearing to be canceled was an error), the police chief sent me a letter of apology for the department's haste in arresting me. Furthermore, the DMV acknowledged the mistake and fixed my license problem. With my submissions to the court concerning the charges against me but now with these facts, my citation was thrown out, my honor restored, and my record cleared. My driving habits slowly improved after that, although it took a few more tickets prior to me learning to ease up on my foot a little.

·     ·     ·

## ... AND EARTHLY MARRIAGES
## SEPTEMBER 1995

I got down on my knees and kissed the ground when I landed in Madras, wiping away joyful tears. Two years after I'd left India, I was back in my home on an official business trip. I did not realize how much I missed the country until we landed. The flight back home was more exhilarating than arriving in New York when I first landed in the U.S. Although my work trip was to cities a few hundred miles away from home, I went for one weekend to visit Hyderabad.

I hadn't told my family about this trip to India. I wanted to surprise them. The big problem was that while Meena was in Hyderabad, my mother, Deepa and Sasi were in different places. Chinni Akka, Bobby and most of the cousins and uncles I would be keen on meeting were in Vijayawada.

To overcome this logistical nightmare, I notified Meena that my boss was visiting, and would be in Hyderabad on a particular date, Friday evening, and requested her to accompany my boss until her departure. She was to be picked up from the airport only by Meena. Our reservations were at a fancy 5-star hotel. Before heading to the hotel, I asked that my colleague stop over at Meena's home for dinner, where she could meet with everyone and enjoy a fine home cooked meal. Then I called my mother, insisting that she and my sisters visit Hyderabad as well. She was hesitant and unsure about having to socialize with an American. I assured her that it would be fine, and we could show off our Telugu hospitality.

As I was waiting for my first glimpse of Meena, my heart was pounding, skipping beats intermittently. When I finally saw her for the first time in twenty-six months, I was hiding behind a massive column at the airport waiting area while she paced back and forth, worried she somehow had missed my boss. I watched her lovingly for several moments, before quietly sneaking up behind her, and gently tapping on the shoulder.

It was the greatest surprise of her life. Unable to contain her excitement, Meena broke down into joyful tears, giving me a tight, warm hug, and a memorable soft kiss on the cheek. Simple romance at its best and I thought once again how lucky I was to have found her and made her part of my life. She wouldn't let go of my hand the whole ride back to her home. While it was wonderful to see Meena and my family; I knew I was here on a mission.

Every other conversation with key family members turned to finding prospective matches for Deepa. I kept rejecting everyone they felt would be appropriate. I wanted to find someone capable of working hard and emigrating to the U.S. I did not approve of anyone from the countryside, as they likely couldn't fulfill such expectations; instead, he had to be an educated, working, humble, family-oriented person. In the end I did not really think that those basic qualities were not too much to ask for at all.

During these conversations, my mother mentioned one match that I had not been told about. The parents were acquaintances of Rao Tatha and had been thoroughly vetted as a family. They were keen on pursuing an alliance with our family due to their great regard for my grandfather. The main problem was that the groom, Mohan, was six years older than Deepa and was working abroad in Nigeria. He had a good character and known as a friendly, industrious young man, who was supporting his family back home.

My family had thought it better if the groom was only three or four years older than the bride and had a more established family, and as a result did not pursue this match earlier. Everything about Mohan, other than living in Nigeria, was music to my ears. Every negative for them was a positive for me. The age gap being slightly bigger didn't bother me, it just meant Mohan was likely more settled, more mature.

"There's nothing better than a self-made person," I argued. When we heard the groom was on vacation in India, we requested to meet him immediately, the same day, if possible, given my tight schedule. But he was 400 kilometers away in another city, having left Hyderabad just the previous night, so we settled for a phone conversation.

My call with Mohan left me with a positive impression: he was delightful, articulate, with a good head on his shoulders. He had a hardworking attitude, a friendly personality, and a great sense of humor. He was willing to go work as an engineer and brave the difficult situation in Nigeria to seek a better life for his family. He clearly told me what he was seeking in his partner, his outlook toward work and life, his responsibilities towards his parents and two sisters. He wanted to get out of Nigeria where armed robbers entered foreigners' homes, stealing anything available.

I could identify with his outlook and—while singing praises of the U.S.—encouraged him to consider moving there someday. We had an hour-long conversation. I managed to track down a couple of people who went to college with Mohan; they gave glowing references. I knew

I'd found the right person after months of attempts and rejections. He had the maturity to balance Deepa's cut and dried attitude. I really thought it would be a perfect fit and he thought my sister suited his criteria for a bride. Seeing my confidence in Mohan, Mother and Deepa became convinced, willing to go along with my judgment.

Given my work commitments and inability to meet him in person, the next steps were left to the rest of the family. My mother agreed to have both the bride and the groom's horoscopes matched by a trusted astrologer. From my mother's traditional standpoint, the stars had to align to ensure heavenly blessings even for these earthly marriages. Few Indian weddings go forward without the blessings of a learned astrologer.

My unplanned visit to India sponsored by my company seemed like it was meant to be. Without my having been there, we would not be ready with my sister's marriage only three months before my own wedding. I was very hopeful that I had found a match for Deepa.

Meena's parents allowed her to accompany me on the rest of my trip. This showed their level of comfort and acceptance of us (And was possibly since our wedding was just weeks away.) We spent five wonderful days in Bombay. Leaving her at the airport was painful, but the thought of me coming back in a few weeks to get married lessened its pain.

Within a few days of my arrival back in the U.S., the groom's family formally met with ours back in India allowing both Deepa and Mohan the opportunity to meet in person and spend time together. Deepa consented to the wedding after that meeting. I somehow knew Mohan would like her, just from the conversation I had with him. Both families agreed to the wedding following a quick engagement ceremony. Hearing the good news, I called my mother and urged her to pull out all the stops for the wedding. The only sticking point was the date.

As much as I wanted to go, I could not get any time off. My family wanted a date that would allow my participation, but Mohan had to leave for Nigeria before I could get back to India. This marriage was on the verge of falling apart over my inability to get there. After much pleading to Deepa that marrying a caring person was more important than my presence, she reluctantly agreed. I sent all the money needed for the wedding, the gifts, the gold, the cash.

For ages, starting when India was one of the richest cultures in the world, in addition to land, gold played an important role in the transfer of wealth. Somehow Indian society has remained obsessed with this custom of displaying one's wealth with gold, diamonds, and other precious jewelry. The bulk of this has a primary role during weddings or religious festivities, making India the highest global consumer of gold in the world.

Deepa's wedding took place in November with over 800 guests at our village home in Vundrajavaram. Widows can't give away their daughters in a wedding, so a close family member takes the parent's place. My mother asked Krishna uncle and Satya auntie stand in for my mother and deceased father for the Hindu wedding's, *Kanyadanam* ceremony. Mohan left for Nigeria prior to my arrival, and my sister stayed behind in India to go to my wedding. I did not meet my brother-in-law in person until several years later.

Just a few days after Deepa's wedding, my mother decided it was necessary to have a traditional, formal engagement ceremony called *Nischitartham* at Meena's home, with a *puja*[9] and other rituals prior to my marriage, where both families exchange vows to solidify the commitment, prior to the wedding. Traditionally at this ceremony the couple's horoscopes are matched to find the best date and time, the *Muhurtam*, for their wedding. The engagement ceremony is a precursor to the wedding. While the groom's mother presents the bride with jewelry and wedding-related clothing, it is also an opportunity to introduce the extended families.

This new wrinkle with plans for a formal engagement ceremony caught Meena's parents off guard, especially because I was in the U.S. and couldn't really take part in the ceremony anyway, but they agreed not wanting to offend my family. I didn't want to have the ceremony in the first place, but my mother was committed to it happening. She wanted all the traditional wedding practices for her only son's marriage,

---

[9] *Puja*, meaning prayer ceremony in Telugu

and the entire extended family were to be invited. After failing to change her mind, and unwilling to push her too much, I relented.

Based on conversations Meena's family had earlier with my mother, Raja Babai, and others, they had planned for a December 1st wedding. Unfortunately for me and the cause of family harmony for no particularly good reason, Raja Babai's second son's wedding had been set for November 29th. After my family found out they consulted with our astrologer about my December 1st date and requested some suitable alternates, perhaps a week distant from the beginning of December. Their intent was to not inconvenience the larger extended family by them having to attend weddings just two days apart. Our astrologer picked December 5th as the alternate date. My family communicated this date change from December 1st to December 5th to Meena's parents. They did not seem bothered by it at the time and willing to accommodate the change by promising to review it with their astrologer. My family took that as a tacit yes and thought it was resolved.

I found out in almost the worst way possible that it was anything but resolved. Apparently, Meena's family astrologer said our horoscope-based star alignment was questionable and so December 5th was not as good for us as December 1st. And that it too had to be at a certain auspicious time on the 1st, adding that getting married on a different date or time could lead to marital problems. Families in India wouldn't hesitate to walk away from wedding plans when predictions like that are made.

At the astrologer's insistence, her family made Meena perform a 30-day ritual where she slept on a floor mat and attended daily temple services throughout the designated period. This was believed to be the solution to the mismatch. Although neither of us have faith in star alignments over our deliberate choices, but we didn't want to hurt her family's feeling or risk their ire. Meena did not want it to become a big deal, especially since my family's request was simply over a matter of convenience. She called me the day before the engagement ceremony and convinced me that I needed to do something. I convinced my mother that night we should let Meena make the choice for her wedding date and keep it as planned, my mother reluctantly agreed.

Unfortunately, during the engagement ceremony my family again broached the subject of changing the wedding date. At this point Meena's hotheaded grandfather made an insensitive remark to my mother, "You should decide if it's more important for you to get your son married at the most auspicious time on December 1st, or if it's more important to pick another date as per the conveniences of your extended family. If some of your family cannot attend, they won't. And if they think attending your son's wedding is important, they will. On top of it, I am not sure why you are insisting on this change now, as your son already agreed to keep this date with Meena late last night and he did not want a change any longer."

This sharp rebuke caught my mother totally off-guard and brought involuntary tears. Seeing my mother crying then upset my family, and it looked like World War III was brewing. A couple of equally short-tempered family members on my side could not keep their cool. They said, "How dare this happens to a widow, in the middle of her son's engagement, how inauspicious is it to make her cry, what sort of a family would do that, and that too the bride's family? No way this is to be tolerated."

But Meena's grandfather wouldn't take back his comments or back down from his insistence on keeping the date. Some of my family decided they should stop the engagement and walk out. Meena's parents were dumbfounded. My mother had not meant for this to take such a wild turn. Luckily for me, Raja Babai quickly read the room and saw the rising level of stress and managed to smooth things over, convincing my mother to back down. My family would go along with everything to ensure successful weddings, even if only two days apart. So, after all the noise and nonsense we went forward with the wedding on the original date of December 1st.

Once again things were not as finalized as they might have appeared. After returning from the engagement, my family was still upset at my mother's treatment. Meena's grandfather's words kept echoing through their minds. He had said that I had quietly agreed to the date with Meena? Then all their anger turned towards me.

"How dare you do this?" They said it meant I don't care for them anymore, or my family's dignity, I must have lost all my self-respect, anxious to marry my sweetheart. Is such a marriage even worth it? I should cancel the marriage rather than marry into a family that wouldn't hesitate to insult my mother, don't I owe my mother more than that? One went so far as to suggest I marry someone else he thought far more suitable from a wealthy family, and he was sure my U.S. professional situation would attract me other top-level matches.

Within hours after their return, I started getting calls from India, everyone had to say their piece. I listened to it all, my anger rising. Immediately I called Meena very upset and sort of just went off on a bit of a rant. But then I also knew I couldn't give in to my family's temporary emotions, and that they didn't mean what they said. When things cooled down, I knew I could talk some sense to them. I called my mother and told her how upset I was at the turn of events. My family wasn't really thinking about what they were doing, with the date change and destructive nature of my family's pride. I added that it didn't help that when my cousins had heard about the situation, they said I would end up as a hen-pecked husband, if I wasn't careful. For several weeks, I spent many sleepless nights on very expensive long-distance calls trying to sort out the whole mess and make the wedding happen.

Five years after we first met, including the two and a half years of painful separation we endured, Meena and I were married, I was twenty-four, and she was twenty-two. Unfortunately for tradition, due to the tightfistedness needed to pay for all the weddings I was responsible for, I didn't get Meena an actual wedding ring until our tenth anniversary. After the engagement fiasco, I tried my best to convince my mother that a small, intimate wedding with close family and friends would be fine. but that was not going to happen.

Her U.S. educated son's marriage was to be the talk of the village. No one had expected my family to get by after my father's death, so she wanted to invite everyone. The main ceremony was in a coconut grove at Meena's family's country home. About 1500 people came for the three-day celebration. None of the extended family missed it, as originally feared, they were mildly inconvenienced due to two weddings within our family, but they found their way.

Fifteen-hundred guests sounds like an impossible number and it was not that my mother or my in-laws knew that many people but there were social expectations that had to be met, as usual. Culturally weddings had evolved to include into not just the bride, the groom, their parents, but the siblings, close cousins, grandparents, uncles, aunts, all other key family members, as well as inviting those that are important in their personal, professional, or business lives. The invitation is a gesture seeking everyone's participation in the festivities and blessings for the couple, in addition to the family's opportunity to dazzle their guests with a big ceremony. While those that are invited feel obligated to attend, non-invitees can get offended. This means weddings have mushroomed into huge convention-center-filling, economy-driving, rock-star extravaganzas.

Our wedding was one of the most colorful and joyful, celebrations without much pomp and show, it was vibrant with mantras and ceremonies, culminating in the tying of a sacred thread with three knots called *Mangala sutra*, representing the elements of our heritage. It was one of the most memorable days of our lives.

Meena and I were at last together. "Tell me you will never stay apart from me ever again like you did the prior two and half years," Meena asked, after our wedding, the first chance we had alone.

"I promise, we will never be separated ever again" I said, gently pulling her towards me.

After my wedding, my mother quickly looked past the engagement incident and bonded with Meena's parents and grandparents as family. But many of my cousins and extended family including Chinni Akka and her husband could never get past that indiscretion. They held me responsible for damaging my family's status, their dignity, and gave Meena a cold shoulder, only warming up after getting to know her. Perhaps some of it was due to distance, while some of it was due to this incident or my imagination of the aftermath of it, but my relationships with Raja Babai's family changed after that for many years, and there was little I could do about it. Finding myself slowly distanced from Chinni Akka, Venkat Anna, and all of Raja Babai's family, my adopted family, with whom I'd grown so close to, saddened me deeply for many years.

Following our wedding, we secured Meena's spousal visa, and she had an approved GA position waiting for her, thanks to my campus contacts. Two days before our scheduled departure, we sent Deepa off to Nigeria, to be with Mohan. Ever since Deepa's match was finalized, I caught some veiled rebukes about the dangers of that country from many in the family, including Chinni Akka. To some extent my mother and Deepa seemed to have agreed to everything—having faith in my judgement, nervously mindful of some of our family influencers' negative opinions about my choice. I was fighting my own feelings as though it was my decision against the world.

That evening after sending Deepa off, overcome with emotions pent-up form all the pressure I had been under, I locked myself in a room and sobbed. No one ever expected me to be so upset, having been sent away from home so young and visiting them once a year during the summer break. I hadn't even grown up with my sisters, how siblings usually grow up together.

So why all the emotions over Deepa's travel to Nigeria? Was it the invisible bond Deepa and I shared, or the weight of the life choices I'd made for her, or the satisfaction of fulfilling a part of my promise to my father? Maybe it was just a momentary lightening of the heavy burdens I had carried, churned up by the uncertainty of what the future held for her with Mohan in Nigeria. After a short four weeks of hectic activity in India, Meena and I headed back to the U.S. in January 1996, embarking on a new and exciting part of the journey of our own lives.

.    .    .

## $5,000 AND THE PROMISE OF A CAREER
## JANUARY 1997

A year after both weddings, I was itching to arrange for Sasi's marriage, while trying to advance my career and establish a better footing to settle down to meet my $300,000 goal, the ambitious target I set for myself when I initially embarked on my journey to U.S. Around then, Meena's uncle, her mother's youngest brother and his wife, expressed a desire to come to the U.S. I decided to help them through an employer within my network. I always felt that having a large social circle in the U.S. helped alleviate some loneliness. Additionally, I saw all the economic opportunities available here, so I felt helping a family improve their life by emigrating was something I wanted to do. Luckily for them, everything came together in a few months and by early 1997, the family of three had relocated to Michigan, initially spending a few weeks with us getting used to their new country.

I joined my company two years earlier while finishing my master's degree in technology. One day, out of the blue, they promoted me and asked if I would be willing to move. They had bought a small manufacturing unit in Lancaster, South Carolina, with plans to build a new facility nearby. I would have moved to Timbuktu if they asked.

Meena and I had no children, and she could still finish her master's degree in Michigan. That allowed us to move without worrying too much about abandoning school or careers. In Michigan we lived in a large apartment with a lovely balcony overlooking the Huron River. To leave all we had to do was turn in our notice, and get it done.

We decided we could stand staying apart for four months on and off while she wrapped up her final term at the university so I could get my job started. We had spent two and a half years separated by 8,500 miles, prior to our marriage. We had vowed to never be separated from each other ever again as those were very painful times for both of us. But here we were once again, lured by a small sum and a good career opportunity—we knew we would have to break that vow. Nothing could stop us from getting ahead, not after everything I suffered from separation and death in my childhood days just to get this far. We didn't realize there were many such separations and further significant pain to endure in years to come, all in search of finding what I thought was a better life.

Unaware of what was in store for me, I drove south by myself in my beloved late model Honda. I had my six-inch white Casper, the Friendly

Ghost figurine on the dashboard. The friendly ghost inside me was driven by others' plight and its eagerness to help with advice and support. When someone gave it to me at a dollar theater, I was attracted to its innocence and couldn't bring myself to get rid of it. I saw it as a good sign. A friendly ghost handed to a friendly guy like me. Dozens of others were given the same thing, but I was conveniently oblivious to that. I smiled and stuck it on the dashboard before my trip. It stayed for the next five years, a happy reminder for me, and a conversation piece for others.

I was 25 when I got to South Carolina during February 1997. I spent my first two days at the only motel in town and then moved into a short-term rental apartment. It was a space in an old house in a small town. My 80-year-old land lady lived in the main house. I had a furnished bedroom, bathroom, a small kitchen and living room combo to myself. The carpets, the bed, chairs, table, fabrics, everything was musty. The place wasn't great, but my land lady was kind and often brought me sweets and cakes.

I found the people always cheerful, displaying fine southern hospitality with deep drawls and broad smiles. Everyone sounded so different or maybe it was the "aliens" like me that were different. The community was pretty, clean, and new. Of course, it was part of the New South. But still, no one wanted to move here not that long ago, as the turbulent social history was still very present. Especially if one paid attention and saw all the trappings of the dominant social order on display.

Not much from here seemed to be top shelf but I relocated, nevertheless. For someone like me that didn't have much to lose, it didn't seem to matter. But I believed it was the hard worker in me that brought me here just as it got me from India to America. They say every city, every region has its vibe. This one had an uncool, predictable, second level, monotonous laidback feel to it. As far as I could tell, there were only two things that were the best around here.

There was a church on every corner. All the roads seemed to lead from one church to another church. Perhaps the only thing that stopped a new church at any given intersection was if one of those, as some saw it, usurping immigrants beat them to it and put up a gas station instead. And the way they sold gullible aliens like me on this unique feature of the Carolinas was that it was a great place to raise a family. They could have told me anything. I would have taken it.

Seemingly without much anxiety, I was excited about the career and the opportunity to have a great life. Meena and I convinced ourselves we would be on the right path in such a family-friendly place.

The other positive thing about the area was the low cost of living. It felt like there was little cost and a lot of living. One's dollars went far; they went so far that sometimes you worried you were getting a whole lot for nothing like you were stealing. This economic feature was slowly attracting a lot of money conscious, family-minded folks like us.

The low cost of living in the area kept me from getting a pay raise, my company initially told me, although it was a promotion. I almost fell for it at first after a feigned intense back and forth discussions with my boss and his boss. They didn't want to give me an increase, maintaining I was lucky to have the opportunity to move to the sunny Carolinas with its inexpensive family-friendly atmosphere.

I was then told I was offered the job because of my talent but they threatened to rescind the offer if I pushed back too hard. My boss threatened that he would give the job to my Chinese colleague who had two master's degrees. What my boss did not realize was that I already knew he was offered it and had turned it down. With this information in hand, in the end I was able to squeeze a $5,000 raise and a new title.

I wore my work ethic on my sleeve, never taking days off, no sick days, no casual call-in days, other than the customary official holidays. That particular year, I convinced my company to combine two years of paid leave for my travel to India in December, hoping for Sasi's marriage to be arranged by then. Taking any time off during my commutes back north wasn't an option. As a result, they expected me to be at work every Monday morning by 8 am sharp, no matter how I chose to spend my weekends and no matter where I had traveled.

The 650-mile distance was not practical for routine weekend visits. Flying cost $450 round trip if booked four weeks in advance, and considerably more for immediate travel. The budgeter in me could never justify paying for those flights, so I went back to see Meena only when it was economically feasible.

Shortly after living in the Carolinas, I discovered that each week on Wednesday mornings, the local airline had weekend deals for $90-$120 round trip. I had to be fast because they went quickly, and they didn't offer the route I needed each week. It was a crapshoot and a wild surprise for Meena whenever it worked. I managed to snatch six such flights home during those four months, even from cities 150 miles away. At eighty-three cents a gallon, I could drive as far as I needed. I didn't spend more than $800 on all trips combined.

I was so over the top in my stinginess that I refused to buy a couch or a bed and convinced my new bride to sleep on a carpeted floor in our bedroom until we paid off our wedding debts. Once during the height of my saving mania, I vocally returned an expensive bottle of cologne she gave me for my first birthday after we were married. It only served to tick her off enough that she swore never to buy me another gift—a vow she ruthlessly kept for years. The nervous accountant in me could never justify such a purchase while I was trying to cover those expensive flights. Plus, all the planning it took to buy so many tickets in advance was not my forte.

Those were still pre-cell phones and internet days, so Meena and I had endless phone conversations in the early mornings, or late at night when the long-distance rates were reduced. But that only took up so much free time, and I was restless. I was itching to be with people, not isolated on my own during the weekends. Weekdays were busy with work, with my new role at the firm. It was the evenings and weekends that were trying.

Being alone brought back unpleasant memories from my early student days in this country and my childhood away from home. To beat the boredom, I bought some used golf clubs for $20. I started spending evenings with some of the golf fanatics from work at the driving range or playing nine holes at a local public course so I could delay getting home, trying to avoid the loneliness and the mustiness. Even after all that golfing over the years, I was a hacker, at best.

Some colleagues occasionally took pity and invited me to their homes. Most of the guys I hung out with and played with were factory workers, supervisors, and managers. I marveled at the time, at the possibilities in this country, where an hourly employee could afford to play golf and live in a decent home that they owned.

While I was a tight wad, spending time in the company of friends and family was something I never took issue with. I was trying to build relationships I believed in, channeling my inner gift of gab. Unlike many of my friends who didn't like eating out, I thoroughly enjoyed every meal I went out for. Being my own sort of foodie, I could straddle from the more delicate end of the spectrum while enjoying all the greasy spoons as well. It is the taste and overall experience that I cared for and a relatively clean, serving environment.

If I was in a place with sticky tabletops, I'd just rest my elbows and arms on paper towels and get on with it. And I wasn't one to have all sorts of food exclusions either. An apt descriptor for my food sensibilities is semi-clean-freak-omnivore. So being on my own didn't impact my food habits at all. Eating out did not necessarily cost a small fortune either. I had a keen eye for deals and early-bird specials; I used every opportunity to save a penny.

Visiting my colleagues' homes, together with some encouragement from them, gave me the idea of buying a home. After some initial deliberation Meena and I put it off and decided to find a small apartment closer to the city. But as was my way, I wouldn't let it go. I was only in the country for three and a half years, two and half years into my job, with little savings for a down payment and negligible credit history. Nevertheless, I decided to dig deeper.

When I went to open my bank account I was introduced to a friendly local banker. These southern bankers are the best, most friendly souls. He said that I could qualify for a loan if I could provide a 10% down payment on a starter home. In the small town, Lancaster, where I was employed, homes were cheaper and larger, and the taxes were dramatically lower. But I could not live there as Meena was planning to work in Charlotte, forty miles away as soon as she joined me. The homes were much more expensive with higher taxes and out of our price range, especially the ones convenient for commuting. Or we would have had to settle for older structures, something we did not want to take on, given our lack of experience with homeownership.

I foolishly tried convincing her that she should commute to the city, Charlotte, forty miles away in exchange for the bigger home we could buy in Lancaster if we successfully got over all the banking hurdles and found a down payment. I got a serious side-eye from her. The fact that it was out in the boondocks meant my arguments didn't have much strength. So, we decided to find a small apartment and live closer to urban sprawl. Traffic would be non-existent for my reverse commute away from the city. She won.

But owning a home was still too much of an attraction for me, I could never fulfill the joy of homeownership in Michigan, with the higher costs and taxes, at least this early in my life. On top of it, most immigrants like me take years to get to the point of buying a home. It's an unusual thing and exploring such uncharted waters gave me a nice kick.

I stopped hunting for apartments and started picking up every real estate magazine I could. They came out weekly, little booklets with homes listed by area and neighborhood, stacked by the dozens outside most grocery stores. This was the stone age as far as the internet was concerned and Google and other real estate platforms were still years away.

Every opportunity I had, I started touring the various locations that had even the remotest possibility of being acceptable. In no time, I became well versed in everything available in the area. It became my favorite past time to drive around looking at different properties and communities. I also did my best to study the entire home buying and lending process.

Once I felt comfortable with the lay of the land, I hired a real estate agent, Mary Beth, a 40-year-old, fun-sounding lady with a bob haircut. Two facts I will always remember about her was that she had never seen the inside of an airplane, and the furthest she'd ever traveled was Georgia and Tennessee.

One weekend, we managed to find cheap tickets in reverse, so Meena could join me instead of me making the trip. My colleagues used her visit to expose her to southern hospitality, so there were multiple invitations to their homes over lunch, dinner, or drinks. In public places, everyone mistook her for the new doctor in town. Mary Beth managed to arrange a few showings of homes, and we trotted around a 20-mile area exploring possibilities.

I knew Charlotte was out of my price range, while the smaller towns were not too interesting. I was determined, nevertheless.

There was one intersection I stopped at every time I drove to Charlotte—just a school zone flashing light, followed by a stoplight at a no-name intersection. The closest thing to civilization was a large, dated red brick high school building. The nearest gas station was a few miles away. There weren't many homes along that stretch of the road within a five-mile radius. I always wondered, "Why was a school here?"

I soon realized this area was in a sort of no man's land. It was the northernmost section of one county, thirty miles from Lancaster, and too far for any of the county services. It was therefore serviced by another town from a neighboring county, still fifteen miles away, but closer than the rest. It was almost a bastard child of either county. That's how most of the area felt. But it had that school building. My entrepreneurial mind told me that if the area developed, it could be a prime spot due to the school and four-lane road infrastructure already in place and given its proximity to Charlotte.

I took a map of the area and drew a one-mile radius around that little intersection next to the school building and enthusiastically called Mary Beth to announce that's where I wanted to live and that our mission was to find a home in that immediate area. Generally speaking, immigrants like me wouldn't live in this sort of area because it was isolated, with woods and farmland and wildlife as neighbors, but that didn't matter to me, if we bought something reasonable in that area.

Meanwhile, I started discussing my official household move down south with my company, about six to eight weeks after I arrived in the Carolinas. Per the terms of my offer and agreement, they were willing to provide professional movers. But I had very little of value to move. Most of the stuff I owned, minus the new bed we purchased after paying off all those wedding debts, a small sofa, and a glass top table with wicker chairs, could be simply sold, discarded, or easily moved. I planned to convince my boss that I would handle the entire move on my own to save the company the hassle of coordinating all that, and they would pay for it.

After several days of dilly-dallying, my boss finally agreed to reimburse the costs and advised me to work with HR to get a few quotes to figure out the reimbursements process. The moving quotes are usually based on the apartment's size, the truck needed, and the distance. Unfortunately, given that the condo we had was a rather large one, the moving company quoted quite a hefty amount for one that big, without ever visiting it. They wanted $6,500.

I had been trying to figure out how to make the down payment for a while. I needed at least $5,000. I convinced my company to pay me the moving costs directly instead of paying the moving company. And that would serve as a down payment on the home. My idea was to find a house for around $100,000, make the down payment, and use the rest towards gas and incidentals for the move. I managed to get the banker to approve my application with as little down payment as possible, thanks to my job and credit rating, I really felt like an American. Now all I had to do was find the home.

# PART III

## STARTING THE NEW AND ENDING THE OLD

*A gift is pure*
*When it is given from the heart*
*To the right person*
*At the right time*
*At the right place*
*And when we expect nothing in return.*

*– The Gita*

# 8

## Two Weddings and a Funeral

### CHAMPAGNE TASTE, BEER BUDGET
### SUMMER 1997

T HE VAST OPEN FARMLAND across from our first house, with hay bales and grazing cattle brought memories of my idyllic, lush green village in India. Our house was a lovely brick ranch style home that was built eighteen months earlier on over 3/4 acre of land. It was on a quiet road near a lonely intersection with a gas station and the school that I took notice of previously. Of course, there was not one, but two churches on the corner of the street. The house was attractive with brick construction, polished wood doors, and a nice front porch with white railing. When we first saw it, we wanted to buy the house. The only problem was the price, $114,000 and it was more than I could pay, but I didn't want to give up on a place we loved.

I drove by every chance I got for several days, three to four times a day. The more I saw it and drove through the surroundings, the more I fell in love with it. My realtor, Mary Beth was skeptical, but submitted my offer of $100,000, which the sellers rejected and didn't even counter. Left with no alternative, we increased the offer to my maximum, $108,000.

I asked Mary Beth if there was a way for me to speak to the sellers directly. She rebuked me, "It's the agent's job to be the communication channel between both parties, the seller's agent would not welcome such direct contact either and the deal may never happen anyway if the seller got upset by this."

On the way to the airport to catch my flight to Michigan that week, I stopped at a gas station and checked the telephone book and tracked the seller's telephone number. I had their name from some paperwork and matched it with the address. I called and left them a message, introducing myself and asking if we could talk. I left them my contact details, hoping they would call. The next day, an older gentleman returned my call. I gave him a brief background of myself and asked for a face-to-face ten-minute conversation.

When I got to the house, I was met by a retired couple working in the garden. They were warm, welcoming folks with big hearts. After exchanging the customary pleasantries and a few details of my trip, why I was traveling back and forth, they invited me in so we could sit and talk.

It turned out that just a year into their retirement, their only daughter developed a serious medical condition. This meant they were driving 250 miles a week to care for their grandchildren. After a while of this they decided to buy a house nearby rather than travel back and forth.

I was surprised at how open they were with their story and their reasons for selling. Peoples' real-life stories always move me, and it felt like we connected with each other. I was hoping that my respect for them, their age, and their situation was evident, in my tone and demeanor. It was clear they loved the home from all the work they had put into it.

I told them about my reasons for moving, our journey thus far in our quest for education and a better life. We were in our mid-twenties, even younger than their daughter. In the same way I understood their story, they seemed to connect with our situation. It was ironic that what was built as their last home, would be our first.

As we were speaking a solution came to me. "None of us know the real value of a home, so I'm willing to purchase at whatever it appraises for. If it appraises for the same or more even, I will raise the additional funds somehow. But if it appraises for less, I will get it at the appraised price." They said this was the most unusual offer they'd heard. I asked them to sleep on it and get back to me. By midday Monday, they called me at work, agreeing to my proposal. I called Mary Beth to tell her what had transpired.

Within a week, the appraisal came at $104,000. The sellers kept their word. That was right in the range I was able to afford. Other than pictures, Meena had not seen the house until we moved in. My mother was so proud of me for having settled into my own home so early in my life. Some colleagues offered to help unload and unpack when we arrived. One of them even showed up with a tool kit and before the end of the night, the bed and kitchen table were assembled, the sofa was in the living room, and everything was hanging in the closet.

We were ready to start our new life in our new home that we owned. We named it *Maitri*, meaning friendship and benevolence in Sanskrit. After that, every house we lived in we tried to create the same feeling, opening our home and our hearts, just as my parents had done with their home in India.

When we started getting furniture, everything we liked was too expensive, "You have champagne tastes on a beer budget," everyone joked. No matter how much we liked a piece though, I was reluctant, unwilling to splurge, as every penny saved was for Sasi's wedding. Less than four years earlier, I was struggling to put together $5,000 just to visit the U.S. and pay my tuition, but here I was just a short while later, realizing The American Dream. Could one be any happier, could a country be any nicer, its people any better? Isn't this what the promised land of opportunity is supposed to be? I was more satisfied with my life than I ever had been.

·    ·    ·

## IMPROMPTU ALLIANCES
## DECEMBER 1997

We'd been saving everything we could for Sasi's wedding. So, movie nights were at the dollar theater, and restaurant outings were to places we had coupons for. We only took short weekend trips, and essentially everything else was on hold.

When Meena first arrived in the U.S., I tried to be her driving instructor, hoping to save money. But that did not go well. It was the first time we lost patience with each other. In what now sounds like a scene from a comedy, one day in the middle of the lesson in the middle of the street she slammed the brakes, got out, and walked home. No amount of pleading to get in the car made any difference. Hearing this, a close friend who had more patience and common sense, came to our rescue and thankfully took my place.

When Meena and I first became close, she liked my outgoing personality, she saw me as loud, funny, and full of life. I went out of my way to take care of my family, so she thought I might be willing to help her family and have the same consideration for her mother and sister. In her mind, it was clear that her father had no plan for his daughters, and they were left to figure things out themselves. She hoped with my help she could steer her family in the right direction.

Through letters and later phone calls, I became closer to her sister Radha over time. I truly thought of Radha the same as my own sisters. I was fond of her vivacious energy. I thought it would be great if I could find a way for her to come to the U.S. to be closer to us. Meena had an engineering qualification which was in great demand in the U.S.; it was expected she would do well there, so her family encouraged her to go abroad. However, Radha wasn't professionally qualified, and her family never expected that sort of opportunity for her.

Back then, wealthy brides with similar qualifications stood a chance of marrying a U.S. settled groom, but not middle-class women. Meena loved the idea of bringing Radha to the U.S. and ease the burden of her marriage on her parents. However, Radha never aspired to move here and generally expected to marry someone in their network in India. Both Meena and I convinced her by instilling the confidence that she could do well here and assuring that we would move their parents here if she moved.

Even prior to my own marriage, I enthusiastically decided to find a suitable match for her from within my network entirely on my own, hoping it would help settle matters for Meena's family. I started assessing eligible men and tried to set up Radha's wedding with a couple of my acquaintances, but things did not work out for one reason or the other. In a similar spirit, I was trying to identify potential suitors for Sasi as well. But nothing worked.

By early 1997 my friend Sarat finished his master's and was working. He was a great guy and a close friend, and I felt very strongly that he would be the right kind of husband and son-in-law and fit well into my family. Since my childhood I have seen how close my two uncles Vasu Babai and Raja Babai were, friends first and then later brothers-in-law. This relationship brought the families closer together. Being together in one large family had always been my secret desire and I imagined there would be nothing better than a friend becoming family.

That was very much in my mind when looking for suitors for Sasi and Radha. So, I came up with the notion to try to get them married and then bring them over to the U.S. so we could all be closer to each other. Initially I suggested to Sarat that he consider Sasi or another cousin of mine. When he did not respond positively, I didn't get upset. I took it in stride and consulted with Meena. In a calm and collected manner I told Meena that I would like to suggest that he consider Radha instead, the chances of him accepting were high given his criteria for a suitable partner. Meena was unsure but agreed to go along, and Sarat readily accepted, his main hurdle being his parents' consent. I offered to mediate for both families.

While getting Sarat's consent was the easy part, neither set of parents were in favor of the marriage nor was Radha. Everyone had their concerns and issues, and Sarat started talking to his side of the family. But I wasn't going to let go of something I thought was good for Radha, the family, and my friend.

At first Radha was unsure about everything, even her willingness to marry Sarat. It took multiple conversations between Sarat, Meena and me to convince her that this would work out well all around. Meena's parents weren't convinced, and I had to intervene and twist their arms a little while singing many praises of Sarat. When Sarat's father objected to the size of the dowry, I suggested my in-laws give their money to their younger daughter, and personally called and assured Sarat's father that everything would be fine.

Secretly Sarat and I had an informal pact to appease the elders and that no real dowry would necessarily be exchanged. When Meena's parents fell short on funds for the wedding, I voluntarily made up the difference. When Radha needed cash for her needs, I happily sent what was required. When Sarat needed a timely loan, I was glad to help there too. I was going to see this through, no matter what.

Meena and I were ecstatic when all the parties involved finally agreed to the marriage over a small engagement ceremony formalizing the agreement for a wedding in December 1997. Sarat, who was in the U.S. and couldn't attend his own engagement, sent a beautiful diamond ring for Radha. Meena and I knew that Sarat would shower Radha with attention. We looked forward to a close relationship between the four of us, in this new country and now our new home. I felt happy that my dream of being family with a close friend was going to be a reality. Everyone believed that Radha was lucky: a move to the U.S., something never previously in the cards, could now be real. For a while, I basked in the glory of praise from all corners.

While I did what I did to ensure a good marriage for both Radha and Sarat, and I couldn't have been any happier for them, I did not realize that my desire for having a friend become family may not be important to anyone besides me. Obsessed with my own myopic view I could not see the finer cracks in the relationship between Raja Babai and Vasu Babai's families and how they had to look past things to really make it work. Meena did not realize I was dreaming of a strong bond with her sister, but it may have required a stronger foundation of sisterly connection than they both had.

In his eagerness to avail himself of the opportunity presented to marry a pretty, lively girl that met his criteria for a wife, Sarat could not have realized the additional burdens that would be placed on the friendship between us. It was my dream that led to their marriage. Radha was happy choosing to simply live in the moment. It was as though everyone took it as a matter of fact, as though their marriage was meant to happen and it did, and that was that. We were all 22-25 back then, young, and naive, trying to do the right thing for ourselves and our families.

Back in India, a pregnant Deepa returned from Nigeria to be with my mother at home for her baby's birth. Sasi was close to completing her MBA. During our weekly phone calls my mother would tell me how happy she was to see me doing well. She was content with how my sisters were doing. I would be too, if the folks at home could find a suitable match for Sasi and arrange for the wedding.

Things weren't as straightforward with Sasi as they had been with Deepa. Like Radha, Sasi wanted to remain in India, not marry someone with aspirations to settle abroad. She feared our mother would be alone if all of us went overseas. The fact that Deepa seemed happy in Nigeria despite the environment there did not increase Sasi's interest. There was a disconnect between what I thought best, what my mother was seeking, and what Sasi wanted.

Failing to solve these matters from a distance, we went to India in December.

Meena was looking forward to Radha's wedding and seeing her parents, and I was anxious to see my mother and sisters and attend three more weddings of relatives and other college friends.

December is prime wedding season in India for those who live overseas. Even though there wasn't any potential suitor under consideration for Sasi, I thought it was better to take it head-on while we were there. I met Sasi in Hyderabad when we arrived, and spoke with her at length, explaining my thoughts about her moving to the U.S.

"You would get the best of everything. Once you live there, if you don't like it, you can always move back. But to reject it without ever even experiencing that environment for yourself is cheating yourself of that opportunity." She was concerned about leaving our mother on her own. Just as we did with Radha, I stressed that eventually, if all three of us moved to the U.S., we could bring our mother as well. She had her concerns, but she agreed to consider people that met my approval.

Convincing Sasi was easy, but finding the right groom was not. I started tapping into every network possible to locate a suitable groom. People avoided me for fear of having to endure hearing about my search. A few days after my arrival, I got a list of several prospective grooms.

The day after Radha's wedding I arranged a road trip to go meet every one of them. Off I went with a relative on a two-day adventure, feeling like sports scouts looking for new talent. But nothing came of the trip, the bachelors were not impressive enough for my sister. I was not going to give up yet. We arranged for two meetings with U.S. educated grooms with my sister, but again not good enough for one reason or another.

At one point we were in Vijayawada, where Meena and I had met, to attend Lakshmi Pinni's daughter's wedding. During the ceremony, I stepped out and found my cousin, Ramu Bava, Krishna uncle's second son. We started talking, and the conversation gravitated towards Sasi's marriage, Ramu Bava started searching his memory for people. By then, his wife, sister, and brother-in-law had joined us. In that conversation, they mentioned a relative with a son that met all my criteria.

The young man, Venu, had a reputation for being intelligent, he graduated from the Indian Institute of Technology, India's equivalent of MIT, and worked at a firm in Hyderabad. They suspected Venu wasn't much older than twenty-three, so the parents might not be thinking about marriage for him. Twenty-six to twenty-seven were considered the best age for Indian men to marry.

So far, I loved everything about him. Meeting Venu and his family seemed like a worthwhile effort, even if nothing came out of it. Ramu Bava felt we should go slow and approach this carefully. We should not try to rush things. He promised to make inquiries, telling me something positive would come out of it even in my absence. But I was adamant about meeting with this family, right away. My cousins started making phone calls and found they were just ten minutes away.

Skipping out on the wedding, we crammed into Ramu Bava's car and headed off. They did their best and presented it as a social call. Ramu Bava introduced me to them and after a brief talk, the conversation moved on to their children and education. Venu's mother was proud to talk about her son's accomplishments with us, highlighting his IIT graduation, his recent lucrative job, and more. She really was a great promoter and advocate for her son, and I was getting more sold on him as she went on, even if she had not realized what she was doing!

We thanked them for their time and made mental notes and returned to the wedding. Again, another pivotal moment in my life played out like some screwball comedy. Running in and out of the wedding between courses to track down a stranger to maybe marry my sister was pretty absurd really, but indicative of the pressure I felt. I told Ramu Bava that I really wanted to pursue this and insisted on meeting Venu as soon as possible. I hoped he would be family-oriented.

Although they kept telling me to relax, I could sense my cousins realized my restlessness and felt sorry for my situation as was evident simply from their constant support. This process reminded me of the importance of family. Having been sent away so young I'm sure it made me even more desirous for a close supportive family environment. I also saw that family dynamics are fluid, and nothing is really fated one way or the other, our own actions can matter. These cousins who were bending over backwards to help me were the same ones who gave me such grief growing up.

At my urging everyone made a lot of calls to try to get us in contact with Venu's family. We finally pieced together that his uncle Babji and aunt Ammaji, his mother's brother and sister were the influencers in the family. It would be necessary to convince them of the marriage, or nothing would happen. There were three hurdles, the first one was to even consider the prospect of marriage, the second was Venu and Sasi had to like each other, and the last, the timing of the whole thing.

I convinced my cousins that since everyone was in Hyderabad, it made sense for us to head back to the city. While shaking their heads and muttering under their breath, everyone nonetheless stuffed themselves into two cars and hit the road on the seven-hour drive in search of this young man, leaving Meena in Vijayawada with other relatives.

By the time we arrived late that night, Ramu Bava had a detailed plan for the meeting the following day. I gave them *carte blanche* to lead the discussions, telling them I wanted to meet Venu in person. If that went well, next was for Venu and Sasi to meet just as quickly as possible. My desire was to finalize everything before my return to the U.S. With a few pictures of Sasi in hand, we arrived at Venu's aunt's home by 10 am.

I saw my cousins work miracles, speaking to Venu's aunt and uncle who had not considered their nephew's marriage, and convincing them that the timing was acceptable. And that a marriage with our family was in their nephew's best interest, and she was a perfect match. It was a delicate dance. My cousins must have gained their skills from earlier experiences. It's akin to a waltz; sometimes one leads, sometimes one follows.

Venu was at work, at a reputed IT company in Hyderabad. His uncle called him at his office and asked Venu to take an extended lunch break to come home and meet a guest from the U.S. When he arrived, we chatted comfortably for an hour, just like meeting any new acquaintance, we talked about his college days, his new job, and my own experiences. He was only about a year older than Sasi and a year and a half younger than me, Meena's age. But the way he carried himself with a sense of quiet confidence, his considered responses, and his professorial demeanor impressed me.

I felt he had immense potential, especially if he moved to the U.S. With his qualifications, it would not be an issue. When I asked him why he had not considered going abroad, he said he wanted to support his mother and family, because his father was ill. I liked everything he said, his serious professional potential, and with his personality, which would balance Sasi's bubbly nature, I thought he would be a great fit.

After getting a satisfactory signal from Ramu Bava and me, Babji uncle showed Venu a few pictures of Sasi, asking his opinion.

With an embarrassed look, Venu reluctantly glanced at the pictures and left the room to talk with his family. None of us had doubts Venu liked Sasi's picture. The real issue was what to do next. A few minutes later, Babji uncle told us that Venu felt she was attractive but was not thinking about marriage at the moment. He wanted to remain single for a few years.

My cousins had a side discussion with the uncle and auntie, to convince him to even just meet her. That way if the initial meeting went well, at least, I could return to the U.S. in peace. The wedding discussions could be held later. It was the consent that we were interested in securing.

Venu tried hard to gently wiggle out by saying he was busy with his work schedule and his inability to take a break. But after a little pressure from his family, he relented. That evening we all headed back to Vijayawada, enroute to Eluru, a nearby town. Along the way, we made calls, making the arrangements for the "meet and greet" between Venu's family and ours at a vacant house in Eluru belonging to Ramu Bava's friend.

Sasi was taking her MBA finals at college but was between test days. She was completely surprised at the urgent summons she received to head to Eluru. She protested that she was busy studying. She was told to study until she would meet the groom, she only needed to spare a couple of hours, and a car was already on the way to pick her up. And of course, a trusted relative was sent to have the bride and groom's horoscopes examined by a local astrologer.

The next day, our family attended the meeting and Venu's parents brought their family to meet us at time fixed by their astrologer. Traditionally, it is called *pelli choopulu*, the event where the bride and groom meet for the very first time, in the presence of close family. After both families were introduced to each other over light refreshments, Venu and Sasi were taken by a relative to another part of the house, allowing them to spend some time alone and get to know each other.

About forty-five minutes later, Venu and Sasi shyly returned from their conversation. Babji uncle met separately with Venu to seek his opinion, and I checked with Sasi. Both said they liked each other.

This was a speed date on steroids! Everyone cheered and congratulated each other, teasing Venu and Sasi, who blushed. I shook hands with Venu's family and hugged my mother and Ramu Bava.

Now that the second hurdle was crossed, I impressed on my cousins the need to somehow get them to agree to the wedding in less than two weeks before my stay ended. Ramu Bava had a quiet conversation with Babji uncle. "Why not have the wedding soon, while the bride's brother is here?" he prompted. We assured them of our capabilities to organize a great ceremony, even on short notice, since we had done it before. Convinced that nothing else was going to satisfy me and unwilling to disappoint my cousins, Babji uncle agreed to press on with the matter.

Venu is a soft-spoken, kind-hearted person, with great regard for Babji uncle. We figured that he would honor his uncle's request and be smitten by my sister after seeing her in person. Babji uncle counseled Venu and his parents that an immediate marriage within a week was possible and the right thing to do. "A brother's wish to attend his sister's wedding, having missed one already, should be accommodated. It would be unduly expensive and laborious to travel roundtrip for the wedding later. Why wait that short time? Why not now?"

It paid off—Venu agreed to get married before I left. We were relieved and grateful. Hoping for this positive response, we'd already had our astrologer on standby to promptly fix the marriage date, a week away, on Christmas Eve. In India, although we faced trouble with my own wedding dates, astrologers have a pragmatic approach to accommodate persistent people like me finding the right dates and star alignments. There is usually a small mystical fix for every situation.

I called my cousin, Karthi Bava, Ramu Bava's older brother to make the wedding arrangements for 800. Unable to book a traditional wedding they got a Nawab's[10] palace courtyard in Hyderabad for the wedding. Since this was the last wedding in our family, I didn't spare any expense, splurging even more than we did for Deepa's wedding or mine, making it memorable for everyone, especially my mother and Sasi.

---

[10] *Nawab*, an erstwhile ruler of a princely state in India.

Although Indian wedding celebrations are depicted as colorful with dances and songs, a momentous occasion for the family, and the happiest day for the bride and groom, in reality, they can be some of the most stressful days of anyone's life, given the ritual, custom, and tradition-centric rigor, combined with the number of guests. It's particularly stressful on the parents.

No one other than the priest typically knows the significance of most Hindu wedding customs, but everyone has an opinion, worried about displeasing the gods or their guests. Every family has their own variation on the different customs that have evolved over generations, and they expected their version to be followed. The groom's family notoriously gets their way because of their belief in their dominant social position, but when that family runs into a bride's family with similar notions of status, all hell breaks loose, ironically on an occasion seeking heavenly blessings and balance.

Having experienced the activity around three prior weddings over something as insignificant as using the wrong kind of silver platter for a certain custom or inconvenient date for a ritual, I made things easy this time by taking a broad-minded approach to anticipate, avoid, and overlook many minor unintended "slights" invariably meted out by both families, to ensure a smooth, heartburn-free experience.

At my request, Raja Babai and Saru Pinni took my parents' place to give away Sasi at her wedding. The festivities around Sasi's wedding were something our family cherished and talked about for many years. Along with the relief on everyone's part, I remember most the joyful look on Sasi after the marriage to Venu. Venu's family was giddy with satisfaction over their charming new daughter in law, the celebrations, and my family's attitude.

It wasn't just that day that has left me with a sense of satisfaction. As hilarious as "arranging" both Deepa and Sasi's, and Radha's marriage was, years later, both my sisters, Radha and their spouses were leading successful, happy, and content lives. It shines a spotlight on the ingredients for a lasting marriage. There is the need for commitment and mature thinking, willingness to compromise, hard work, trust, respect, and honest communication to make a resilient relationship. As rushed as I was, it was the personal qualities of each groom that helped me hone-in and make seemingly quick decisions, rejecting potential match after match. The entire family on both sides were overwhelmingly pleased with my ability to help settle the lives of these three young women.

I could not thank my cousins enough for helping with Sasi's marriage, it would not have gone forward without their astute management. My mother's side of the family facilitated Deepa's alliance, while father's side facilitated Sasi's. I was the catalyst. Earlier, one side of the family took care of me for several years at Krishna uncle's home, later another side took me in at Lakshmi Pinni's. It is a blessing to have such a family. Whenever I really needed something, the entire family came together to help. All I had to do was ask. The best and most unique part of India and being Indian is the family.

·　　·　　·

## A ROCKY START
## JANUARY 1998

Meena and I were exhausted after the thirty hours of travel home following a crazy four-week trip. Taking a deep sigh, we held each other's hands and said at the same time as though we could read each other's thoughts. "I'm glad to be back home." But wasn't India our home? We were visitors working in the U.S. that owned a house. How strange that we both felt glad to be home when we just arrived from home. Were we no longer aliens anymore?

For the previous four years, I was obsessed with the thought of my sisters and Radha's weddings. Once I had realized all my initial objectives, it was exhilarating and exhausting, and to some extent confusing, as though I was becoming purposeless now, while simultaneously a sudden feeling of liberation ran through me, realizing that our time and our earnings were finally ours from then on. "What next?", wasn't clear.

Meena had been deferring her own needs this whole time. Of course, all along over the prior few years it was tempting, and we had to resist the urge to buy pricier cars, nicer clothes, take vacations, or spend our earnings lavishly on ourselves. Nothing was worth more than helping our families settle. I trained myself to defer everything, and Meena too, whole heartedly.

My monthly budget prior to my marriage was less than $600, and after my marriage we still managed to keep the household expenses to $1,000. Including Meena's salary, everything we earned went towards saving for the weddings or repaying loans. It felt like we'd just married off our own children. Completely unwilling to take on the responsibility for another person we rejected any suggestions we should have children. Instead, we started thinking about how we wanted to define our lives together and began sketching out long-term plans. Planning is something I thrived on and now that my family's goals had been met, I needed a renewed sense of purpose.

Our first order of business was getting Green Cards for permanent residency. Next it was reaching my goal of $300,000 a year and an MBA. Then, we could still return to India if we wanted to, and Meena and I would start a company of our own. But it was all about building our life with my mother, sisters, Radha, Meena's parents, both sides of our family, bringing everyone together either to the U.S. to visit, and pursuing our careers here or back in India. That's how we imagined our future. Our plan was to try focus on ourselves, personally and professionally. It was time to build the future we could have only dreamt of until then.

A book that piqued my curiosity around that time was about the habits of American millionaires, *The Millionaire Next Door*. We did not realize until then that over eighty percent of U.S. millionaires were self-made. That was so contrary to the wealthy in India who mostly inherit their wealth. They were small business owners, the frugal professionals, the incremental savers. I carefully made notes, debating with Meena about the various scenarios presented. It turns out, I had a what the book called "the millionaire mindset," described as one that will work towards financial freedom people usually only dream about, but don't put in the requisite thought and hard effort into it.

Such self-made millionaires only make up one to two percent of America. They live in average homes in average neighborhoods driving used cars, wearing regular clothes, and inexpensive watches. There is a difference between those who look rich and those who are rich, the research explained. Looking rich seemed fake to me; I'd seen enough of that in India. Living below your means is a core element of this mindset.

Observing my extended family, even the wealthy ones, I only found one family out of a group of forty to fifty that exhibited the "millionaire mindset." Growing up, I intuitively admired that one family for their savviness, but never understood why others around them didn't share a similar outlook, learning from them about living below their means. It was this "Finance 101" that was missing for most of my family. I did not want to end up like that for sure. I decided to do something about it. Real generational wealth is built over a long time, and the wealthy have a habit of preserving their capital, carefully studying, and planning their investments, taking a long view of things.

I read once that a good way to get somewhere in life is to know where you want to go and how you want to be remembered: imagining how my life could unfold, what and who might be in it. I pondered various epitaphs for my tombstone, not that there would ever be one. After toying with the idea of being wealthy as a successful industrialist, or a famous and influential political figure, or varying ideas of material success, being a good son, a good husband, a good brother, I finally settled on one line.

It probably came from a subconscious memory of the *Chandamama* or *Amar Chitra Katha* comics I, along with all the other kids, read voraciously during elementary school. They were short graphic novels in English that depicted Indian cultural heritage through morality tales of stereotypical good vs. evil protagonists. Tales started with some version of "A long time ago a wise king ..." or "An old sage once said ..." or "Once upon a time in the kingdom of ..." I decided on "A wise old man that once lived ..." for myself. It resonated with me: I wanted to live a long life, with health, professional success, happiness, but most importantly, the wisdom to keep it balanced.

I thought of that line whenever I was in doubt. "A wise old man that once lived." That's what I aspired to, however playfully it started. I wasn't sure if I could live up to such a lofty ideal, but it seemed like the right way for me to go.

Meena and I had made an agreement prior to our marriage: we were going to support each other, respect each other, and work hard to make a life for ourselves. We were not to hold back any feelings from each other, and share all the good, as well as the bad. Honesty, respect, and commitment would be the foundation of our relationship.

It doesn't mean that we didn't raise our voices to each other during a heated argument or a discussion occasionally. We would bare our hearts when our tempers got frayed, true to the honesty we promised to practice. But the commitment clause kicked in right behind it, we would never go to bed upset with each other, even if it was 2 am, we would hug, kiss, and snuggle in the same bed, no matter what, or keep the discussion alive and resolve the matter without letting negative feelings fester and dig in.

Often, given the intensity of our arguments and the harshness in our tones, our friends and family thought our relationship was odd. To our chagrin, this had even been predicted by that wretched astrologer before our wedding, that said that we would be anything but in sync. We were the North Pole and the South Pole, he said, just opposites that were never to meet or see the same on any point or subject. We knew several families in India that would reject perfectly good marriage alliances on account of such quirky predictions, and that was the reason Meena insisted on having our wedding date selected by that same astrologer, to reassure her family that all the bases were covered. Of course, he was wrong in our case.

We were just two strong personalities with independent minds, it wasn't that we didn't see each other's views. Neither of us was bothered by such predictions because we had immense regard for each other's values, thoughts, and dreams. We knew we were a low-risk couple. We knew each other well, and to me, that was the foundation of any good relationship.

Once all our debts were cleared by the end of 1998, as the pressure to have children kept increasing, we instead got a German

Shepherd puppy. Growing up on *The Phantom* comics, I imagined saving the world riding a white horse with my trained wolf, Devil, by my side. With these stories in mind, I named this adorable gentle pup Devil, and of course I was the Phantom. We raised him like our child, and he grew up into a loving and attentive friend. He got the best of everything and got to go everywhere we did.

Venu and Sasi moved to the U.S., initially living in the Charlotte area. Venu found a lucrative job, as I thought he would. We were thrilled to host them prior to their settling down. A year later, they moved to Michigan, for an even better job, and Sasi started working at a bank.

Mohan and Deepa began planning leaving Nigeria and returned to India as a first step. Canada seemed to be a good option for them, so they applied to emigrate there. My dreams for my sisters were coming true.

My next goal was to have my mother come over. We could have had her join us sooner, right after Sasi's wedding. But she wanted to wait until I settled all my debt, not wanting to burden me with her expenses. But just as we were preparing for her visit, once again things changed in India that affected us dramatically in June 1999.

My father-in-law was an engineer, and a senior government official managing a large engineering department. He was more than eight years older than Meena's mother, who was married when she was seventeen and had Meena at eighteen, and Radha, a year and half later. Although Meena's father had a good job, just like Krishna uncle, the government salary was barely sufficient.

Meena's maternal grandparents, landowners like Rao Tatha and my family, supported their daughter occasionally. However, the strong personalities of Meena's grandparents and her father were a mismatch, and they didn't see eye to eye on many things as a result. Trouble started shortly after they were married when her in-laws started complaining about her and her family over some long-forgotten slight. Her husband sided with his family, and this seemed to get their relationship started on the wrong foot.

Meena's mother was the darling of her family. She had moved to Hyderabad as soon as Meena was born. When Meena's sister came along her grandparents brought Meena to their home in Eluru, 350 kilometers away. They said they didn't want their daughter to be burdened with taking care of two infants by herself in the city.

Meena lived with her grandparents until she was ready for elementary school. Being the first grandchild, everyone including her three uncles and great-grandparents doted on her. She was a precocious little girl who thrived on all the positive attention. The early years she spent there created a deep connection with her mother's side of the family. She didn't consider them grandparents as much as a second set of parents, and her maternal uncles were like older brothers. Even after she came to the city for primary school, Meena craved the love of her grandparents and uncles. Winter and summer holidays, Meena and her sister went to their grandparents keeping their connection strong.

It was Meena's strong sense of family that attracted me to her early on. As Meena got older, she became aware of the tensions between her father and her mother's family. She would always see the aftermath of one of the family disputes ... her mother in tears, or her father angry. She knew something was wrong but lacked details. Despite the friction between their parents and a certain amount of emotional distance from their father Meena and Radha had happy and loving childhoods.

Meena's mother would supervise their studies and homework but also take the children to movies, parks, libraries, and museums, and play many board games with them. Her father was more reserved and didn't interact a great deal with his children. He was often sent to remote parts of the state spending a lot of time away from home supervising new projects and development programs. He came home on weekends and as his schedule allowed. As Meena became a teenager the tensions within the family got more pronounced and disruptive. Her father would berate her mother and grandparents about what she thought were trivial matters. This happened when someone's ego had been bruised in one way or another.

Over time, these combative feelings kept escalating, reaching a peak when Meena was in high school. At the time her father lost a significant amount of money in the Indian stock market. To cover his losses, he demanded his in-laws liquidate a portion of his wife's inheritance, which they refused to do. They wanted to protect the assets for their granddaughters, Meena and Radha. Reluctantly, Meena's mother sided with her parents. This created an even-greater divide between her and her husband, and more unpleasant conflict in their marriage. I have always thought how much of a tragedy it is that so many relationships end up on the rocks because of financial differences and problems. Once again, I must give credit to my uncle for working very hard to instill in me some very helpful fiscal guidelines to try and live by.

Her mother had often told Meena that women should have financial independence, so they would not get stuck in a situation like hers. Meena was a good student and paid attention to her mother's advice. She made up her mind to complete engineering school and go to the U.S. and work towards a career even before I had met her. Although enthusiastic relatives forwarded multiple possible husbands for Meena as early as sixteen, her mother politely declined, thanking them, and saying that Meena was focusing on her education and career first.

Meena's closeness to her grandparents might have created a rift between Meena and her sister, or maybe it was Radha's own insecurities about her standing in the family. Meena was an "A" student, gentle and sensitive since childhood, and the favorite of the extended family while Radha was left on her own to stand in her shadow.

If there was anything brewing in that relationship between the siblings, it went largely unnoticed. A wonderful family with two adorable girls, supported by an extended family of uncles and grandparents it was perfect to the outside world. As they came of age Meena developed a sober personality with an air of quiet confidence while Radha developed a competitive one with a gregarious nature. Whatever it was, it certainly influenced how they perceived the situation between their parents and grandparents.

Meena thought her father to be weak and needlessly combative, and what bothered her even more was his willingness to harp on his disagreements with his in-laws. Meena sided with her mother and grandparents and Radha sided with her father. Radha developed some resentment towards her grandparents and a soft spot for her father. She assumed everyone was unfairly blaming him. Given this dynamic, Radha became her father's favorite. Although he was proud of Meena having followed him becoming an engineer, anytime these interpersonal matters surfaced, it widened the divide between them.

I was clueless about this dynamic. Based on their interactions and how Meena and Radha spoke of each other and cared for each other, I imagined they were as thick as thieves. Perhaps they were, in everything else but this one matter, I could never tell.

I knew her father had differences with his in-laws, but I did not know the extent of the problem. Meena had been away at college and then in the U.S. with me, essentially away from home for most of the prior nine years. Meena's mother, who was close to her parents, was caught in between her husband and her parents. After Meena got married and left, the situation got even worse. In addition to my financial support for Radha's wedding, Meena's parents ended up acquiring debt to ensure they got Radha the wedding of her dreams, something Radha insisted.

Meena cautioned both Radha and her parents to be mindful of the expenses and that it was still possible to have a good wedding without spending so much. Meena reminded them that while her wedding had been large, we held it at a countryside family farm, where the costs were kept considerably lower. But with Radha's wedding in Hyderabad, it was costing a fortune.

Meena saw her parents struggling to repay their loans after the wedding. As was his habit, her father demanded his in-laws help pay the loan from her mother's inheritance. Frustrated with these developments Meena confronted her mother saying she'd cautioned her about her father, and what he would do to repay the loans. She started decreasing the number of calls to her mother not wanting to hear about the never-ending saga.

A year or so after Radha's marriage the domestic conflict was so great that her mother left the house to stay with a friend in Hyderabad to get some time away. When she heard this news, Radha, who was in the U.S., urged her to return home than stay with the friend a little longer. Her mother went home and as might be expected things did not improve between the parents. Meena was not told about any of this.

A few months later, seeking respite from the conflicts with her husband, she went to see her parents. On the way there the bus had an accident, and she broke her arm. Meena heard about this accident and the broken arm and why she was traveling in the first place. Meena does not care about appearances and knowing her father's combative streak, she wanted to protect her mother. She begged her mother to remain there for a month or as long as it took, until she recovered and for things to cool down at home. But Radha once again urged their mother to return home.

Her mother initially took Meena's advice and stayed for about a week but owing to pressure from her husband and Radha she decided to return. When Meena begged her not to go home, she teared up saying, "I wish I could stay." Meena told me about what was going on and asked me to see if I could do anything to improve the situation. I thought about it a great deal and decided against it because I felt it was too much of an intrusion into their personal relationship. I also thought that it would not be taken as helpful but rather presumptuous, and it was better to let them try to come to some sort of resolution on their own.

The day after her mother returned to Hyderabad, Meena called to wish her parents a happy anniversary. But her mother was at home by herself with her broken arm. Meena asked why she was alone, especially on her anniversary. She told her that the maid had left after preparing some food and helping with her bath.

Meena was upset her father wasn't there and taking care of his wife. She asked her, "Why are you even at the house when there is no one there to care for you, you would be better off at grandparent's house?" In a deeply sad voice Meena's mother replied, "Perhaps you can speak to your dad?" After a little small talk Meena hung up the phone, determined to speak to her father as soon as she could reach him.

A few hours later, on that Saturday afternoon, Meena received the tragic call that her mother had been killed in a traffic accident.

I was not at the house when she got the call. After cutting the lawn, I had gone on some errands leaving Meena home finishing up some chores. Her parents' next door neighbor and close friend, Eshwar, called from India. Hearing Meena's voice, he started to cry, and Meena's heart skipped, "What happened?" He told her that her mother was gone. Meena shut down mentally, "What do you mean, gone?" she asked.

"She was killed in an accident." He replied.

"What accident? You are confused, it was only her arm that fractured. She is fine. I just spoke with her a few hours ago." Meena said.

The neighbor answered, "Yes but there has been another accident. It isn't the same accident you are thinking of."

"No, that can't be true, how can that be, did you check, it must be a mistake, can you get another doctor to check her out?" she pleaded. Then she heard him wailing on the other end of the phone and her world collapsed. This was before cell phones, so she had no way to get in touch with me. She had to inform Radha and her maternal uncle's family in Michigan.

When Meena's mother passed away in the second, fatal accident, on the very day of her 27th wedding anniversary, her right arm was still in a cast from the first accident. With little regard for her condition, her husband had convinced her to visit a friend's home for dinner, they rode together on a scooter with my mother-in-law hanging on the back with her broken arm. Despite his friend's suggestions to not go home after dinner until the weather got better, my father-in-law would not listen.

To make matters even worse, he was inebriated when he decided to drive home through the nighttime drizzle. While they were making their way home a city bus, driving too fast and too close to them on a crowded main street hit them, the bus bumped into the scooter trying to avoid a pothole and caused Meena's mother to fall towards the bus, and her father the other way. My father-in-law escaped largely unscathed, and the scooter remained intact. But my mother-in-law struck her head. At that time there was no organized emergency medical services in India, no calling

911, no ambulance coming in minutes, nothing. By the time the police arrived, her father with some bystanders moved her to the hospital, but it was too late. Shocked and devastated by the news, we rushed back to India.

My mother-in-law's last rites were performed before we even got there. Meena and Radha were not able to see their mother one last time and say a proper goodbye. This is one of the saddest and darkest aspects of the immigrant experience, being so far away from one's family in times of crisis. Lucky are those who get to share time with their families. After ten sorrowful days, we returned to the U.S.

The untimely, heartbreaking loss of Meena's mother, her guide, friend, and rock was very difficult. It scarred her, removing the optimistic smile from her face, silencing her, shaking her faith for a long time. She shut down emotionally.

There's something about Indian culture that when an untimely death occurs one is left to struggle and deal without significant emotional support from the family at large. This is the same thing that happened around my father's death, and no one wanted to talk about that either, or to help console and heal. It is a culture where death is treated as a reward, regarded as "Moksha," a freeing of the soul from its earthly bindings, from the pain and suffering of the human condition. Life was explained away in a philosophically deep but psychologically unconvincing manner with Vedantic language invoking deities for anything inexplicable, citing karma, destiny, or fate as possible reasons to why such terrible tragedies happen. "Everything happens for a reason," and everything in life is the result of past or present actions, your "Karma," one hears all the time in India.

If some say that life is the result of "Karma," I argue instead that: Intent + Karma + Chance = Life. Karma is nothing but our actions and it's the role chance plays, creating new and unexpected circumstances, that makes many things in life impossible to explain and reconcile.

Meena could never get past the accident and forgive her father for the loss. She was upset with Radha for siding with her father and pressuring her mother to return home. She was upset at the underlying reasons and the financial stresses after Radha's marriage that added to the conflict between her parents and grandparents. She was upset that her mother felt compelled to sell all her personal jewelry prior to her death trying to repay their debts. She was upset at Radha for keeping such details from her. Meena and Radha's early sibling bonding slowly transformed into a convoluted and somewhat fraught emotional relationship as adults.

Beyond all the tragedy in her life, her inability to maintain a close bond with her only sibling has always lingered as an emotional regret in Meena's life, and perhaps the same is very true for Radha as well.

As if to add insult to injury, my father-in-law had started talking about remarriage three months after his wife's death and got remarried within a year. They had been married twenty-seven years to the day when she passed away, and it was as though none of that mattered. I would like to think he was a poor communicator and could not express his sadness. I know he wasn't a bad person, just someone caught up in his ego.

Meena could never get past his lack of remorse, the fact that his wife literally died in his hands, through his recklessness, and it did not seem to matter to him. Moreover, when her father visited us prior to his remarriage, he spent three months here. He never told Meena about his impending wedding, but he told Radha. The day prior to his wedding he called Meena and told her that he was getting married the next day. This created a permanent rift between him and Meena. She felt her mother was not being respected even in death by him getting married so quickly. She thought it was just his inability to live alone and do things for himself.

When I suggested Meena perhaps be more considerate towards her father, she got angry saying, "What kind of human does that? This is the person my mother was forced to come back to and lose her life for. And he had the gall to stay at our home for a month without the nerve to tell me to my face. I am not mad at him as my father, but as a person, for the immoral choices he made. I just don't want to associate with him anymore."

Radha again sided with her father, perhaps unwilling to distance herself from the only remaining parent or thinking that his comfort was more important at that point than some external display of affection for their deceased mother. But the fact that neither Radha nor Sarat bothered to inform us about what was happening tore Meena apart. Meena felt, "When people consciously and knowingly make choices and hide them from you, they either know their choices are bad or that it would hurt you, but they still go ahead."

Radha may have feared Meena's reaction or possibly thought she was being kinder to Meena by not sharing the information with her directly, or she may not have wanted to be the bearer of such difficult news. Or was it that she just didn't care? Regardless of the reason she chose to handle it that way, this disagreement widened the gap between the sisters, limiting our contact for a while. Meena never spoke much to her father after that.

Following her mother's death, even with her father alive, Meena felt orphaned and could not bear to go back to India for many years to face a home without her mother. Just like I couldn't fit into my village after my father's passing, she did not see herself fitting into that environment anymore without her mother. India was no longer her home. I could not get her to shed those feelings and open up. Seeing Meena that way saddened me immensely, and her unwillingness to talk about her feelings added to my frustrations.

My earlier dream of the lone warrior returned to haunt me once again over long restless nights. Our earlier plans of returning to India after reaching certain milestones in the U.S. suddenly seemed less clear. India felt even more far away now. To distract ourselves from all these developments, we dove in even deeper into our work.

# 9

## The Calm Before the Worst Storm

### A HONEYMOON, FINALLY
### JANUARY 2000

**M**Y WORK CONTINUED TO CHALLENGE and excite me. The Germans completed their acquisition of our small firm. The parent company was a multi-billion-dollar global conglomerate with unparalleled engineering prowess, popular for its history and success going back a hundred years. After successfully delivering on various critical projects with excellent results, my bosses in Germany selected me to train in German management practices, and then come back to run a larger division. I liked to think it was because of my indispensable talent, but in reality, the Germans seemed to trust my American colleagues the least, so this Indian suited them better.

Ever since my undergraduate experience, I had been dissatisfied with my educational trajectory. I had great promise until high school, and then had come down to average. My course corrected with my U.S.

sojourn. Although I was an engineer, my heart and skill set has always been in management. Pursuing an MBA was the logical step to get a formal education and that degree.

When I broached this with my bosses in early 2000, they told me they wanted to offer me a position in Germany, it would require us living there for three years. The MBA could wait. Going to Germany, getting such an offer was a rare opportunity, it was a significant move for me, along with more exposure to the corporate heavyweights at headquarters. My concerns about the Green Card were quelled with the assurance that it would be processed as planned. Everything a young, career-minded executive needed to hear was said.

Part of me was tempted to sell the house and move completely. We could make the most of living in Europe while soaking in everything I could about the German operations. That's what they expected me to do. But Meena would have to take a break from her career. We decided that the best thing would be for me to reduce the length of the assignment. We could stay apart for a short period. Meena could work while I was in Germany, and I'd visit as often as possible. This was one of those moments, again, for me where success and sacrifice came at the same time. I was lucky to have a partner who had a similar appreciation for professional achievement and supported me all the time. That spring, I arrived in Germany and was given a fully loaded company apartment where even my laundry was washed, and a German sports car.

Towards the end of the summer, Meena came to Europe, and we took off exploring. We had taken other trips, but nothing that could be considered a vacation, until this. Five years after our wedding, this felt like a long overdue honeymoon. No matter when you celebrate, it must be the state of mind, not the timing that makes a honeymoon.

We spent ten romantic days entirely unplanned, driving towards Paris, stopping along the way in Amsterdam, Antwerp, Brussels, and Waterloo. We just wanted to drive to the Eiffel Tower and then find a hotel and stay a few days. As we got closer to the city, the rush hour traffic, and a rainstorm, turned us around. Thinking we may be lost I pulled over to get directions. Looking through the fogged-up windshield, we saw a sign in English.

Leaving Meena in the car, I jumped out of the vehicle head down, hands over my head, protecting my face from getting drenched. Water was running along the street by then, and trying to leap over the water, I landed on one foot, and before I could find a firm ground for my other foot, my face crashed into a glass wall. Through all that rain and fog, I hadn't seen a glass storefront within two feet of the sidewalk. Everything happened in a flash: the entire fifteen to twenty-foot glass wall came crashing down, shattering into little pieces.

I fell into the lap of an unsuspecting customer with blood dripping down my face and arm. Startled, all five or six people in the store just jumped and ran, trying to find safe corners. Hurt and ashamed, I got up, dazed, apologizing. To my relief, the store owner came to my rescue and helped me calm down, sit, and relax, as he gathered cloths to wipe down the blood. After they learned I was okay, the others slowly relaxed and started smiling, asking me questions, in French. I gestured that my wife was outside in a car. They found Meena casually listening to music, completely oblivious to what was going on.

Soon the police and the medics came. After administering basic first aid they transported me to the hospital and Meena followed. After a couple of hours of tests and checks, I could be allowed to go my merry way with some medication, a few stitches, and a bandaged forearm. All along, I kept apologizing to the police, the ambulance medics, the nurse, and finally, the doctor.

Everyone was friendly, amused at the unfortunate mishap, and when all was said and done, they offered me perfect directions to the Eiffel Tower. A few hours behind schedule, and with small laceration on my lip, a visible scar on my hand, and a cheeky smile inside me, Meena and I found the most romantic landmark in the world.

Welcome to Paris! We ended up in a hotel just a block away from the Eiffel Tower. The following week I had to unexpectedly head back to the U.S. again in crisis mode.

.　　　.　　　.

## A MILLION DOLLAR LOTTERY
## FALL 2000

The reason for my emergency return to the U.S. was the status of my Green Card, the permit that allows an immigrant to remain in the U.S. indefinitely, without any visa hassles. My Green Card had been in the system for over six years, stuck in an eternal query loop from the immigration department. The years passed, and it had become a waiting game for one reason or another. I had thought it would be a routine process, so I got a run-of-the mill immigration attorney, hoping to avoid spending too much money. It was anything but fast or routine, and I got very little for the price. After all this time, we had been repeatedly told that everything was in the final stages, and we should hear something any day.

We were hoping to hear the good news that our application was approved while we had been away. Nothing happened. A few days after Meena left, after dialing the automated phone number as usual, I was excited at a change in the status. By then, I'd gotten so familiar with the messaging system that I felt I could sense differences based on the music they played when you were on hold.

Instead of getting good news, I got a message that said my application has been denied. I had a huge knot in my stomach and instantly saw my world falling apart, my professional future shattered, my improving finances ruined. I feared being stopped from going back home. It could take months or more once a thing like this gets stuck in a loop; we'd heard many horror stories over the years. Maybe I would have to go to India first to get another visa of some sort before being allowed to go home. My company wouldn't keep me without a visa and that could force us back to India, which Meena didn't want after her mother's death. I felt like I was choking and sinking, fighting to stay afloat in a capsized boat.

My hands trembled as I picked up the phone to call Meena. "Everything will be fine, don't worry," she said, not showing any sense of disappointment. She didn't seem as perturbed by it as I was. I always admired this cool and balanced nature of hers, especially over such matters. "We'll find a way to work things out. We can move back to India if we have to." She remained calm and tried to assure me.

164

She reminded me that we'd developed a habit of living on one income. It was not just to drive the savings up, but also to avoid getting used to expensive living. But I wasn't prepared to accept things as they were. I had an idea. The risk was worth taking, there was little to lose.

I called my boss in America, Fred, telling him that heading back to the U.S. would be the best move. I called the office in Germany, telling them I was heading home for an emergency, promising further details. The entire flight I kept imagining the worst scenarios of getting stopped at immigration. But when I arrived, the immigration officer merely said, "Welcome back home." It was music to my ears.

I was home, but my problem was not yet solved. Fred was committed to helping me fix this problem, assuring me that he would move heaven and earth to keep me here. I was somewhat relieved. More importantly, Meena and I were together. No matter what was in store for our future, it would be much easier facing it together.

With my company's full weight behind me, we reached out to the congressman for our district. His office contacted immigration authorities, demanding my case get immediate attention. I fired my old attorney and got a lawyer from one of the top law firms in the country. Within thirty days, thanks to my new attorney's appeal and the congressman's intervention, our Green Cards were granted. Just like that, a process that had dragged out over six years suddenly was settled.

It almost seemed like a miracle, and I knew it was a significant step forward for my family's future security. I do not know how it feels to win a million-dollar lottery, but it couldn't feel any better than getting permanent American residency. It was one of the most satisfying and memorable days of my life, removing the layers of uncertainty engulfing us with security and peace of mind. The Green Card is the immigrant's best friend, unlike no other.

After getting my Green Card, I finished the rest of my assignment in Germany, returned home, and was promoted to a senior management position. In early 2001, Deepa, Mohan, and their three-year-old daughter Maya emigrated to Canada, settling near Toronto. Soon after arriving, they both found jobs. At the same time Sasi and Venu were settling well in Michigan.

While our relationship was not exactly stellar due to Radha and Meena's differences, through my active intervention, they made up with each other realizing the need to prioritize their bond over any other matters. We had mutual friends and the fact that all four of us enjoyed each other's company, we all did our best to look past our differences and find common ground. For a while it seemed to work.

We had been meeting often, traveling, taking vacations, and leaning on each other on important personal matters. Once again, I felt a contentment like I had never felt before. My mother was still living in our village in India, but we were planning for her to join us. We had put it off for too long, but because Deepa had moved away from India as well, we felt the timing was right. Thanksgiving and Christmas became real celebrations for our family, not for the religious aspects of it, but rather the festive spirit. We looked forward to the holiday meal of roast turkey and ham, and warm cider for Thanksgiving and putting up a tree and decorations, sharing the holidays with friends and family. We once spent the entire holiday vacation in New York City. We were becoming seriously assimilated immigrants. We also finally secured a visitor's visa for my mother to visit us.

.      .      .

## UNITED FAMILY
## SPRING 2001

The thought of my mother arriving in the U.S. was exciting. I would not have imagined it just a few years earlier. It had been two years since I had seen her, the last time being for my mother-in-law's funeral. In fact, I had only seen my mother on three occasions while visiting India over the eight years I had lived in the U.S. All our communication had been over the phone and through letters. My desire to be with my mother was unfulfilled, seeing her was always elusive for one reason or the other, ever since my childhood, and now she was finally on her way to see me.

I wanted her to be proud of everything we were doing here, our home, our lives, and shower her with as much love and attention as we could. On her first trip we decided that she should fly to Detroit where Sasi was. I bought a brand-new car to drive her to our home in North Carolina from Michigan. The frugal millionaire habits I adopted weren't compelling enough to hold back my urge to impress my mother.

We had a family reunion at Sasi's home. As soon as I saw my mother, I wrapped my arms around her and didn't leave her side for the entire afternoon. To be honest I felt like a child again who was finally seeing my mother after the school year. My mother stayed with us for three months that trip. It was the first time I'd ever spent that much time with her since I was three!

Just as little children question parents about their own childhood, their parents, the family, I took every opportunity to ask her the same sort of questions. She told us about my father, her marriage with him, the loss of her first child, my birth, her grandmother Devamma's impact on her while growing up, her views on life, and reasons for some of the more important moments in the family's life.

My mother reminisced on her upbringing and her life. Born into a wealthy family, being the third of six siblings, she was raised by her maternal grandmother Devamma during her teen years and acquired her piety and outlook on life from her. Her grandmother lost her husband when she was middle-aged and learned to manage the household by herself in a male dominated society. She was wealthy and never had to worry about money. My mother chose to take a similar path when my father passed away, rather than rely on my grandfather, Rao Tatha's support. However, my mother wasn't wealthy, so she struggled with running the household. She did it without getting into debt, sacrificing much, and providing everything for her three children.

My mother and father had a good marriage, excellent compatibility, and cared for each other. He encouraged her to be social and they always participated in social gatherings together. She told us many stories about my father, her lifetime of happy and sad memories. He was a worldly man, known to enjoy the pleasures of life, smoking, drinking, and the like. Socially, he was sought after, his company was always welcome. Had he somehow managed to recover during those final days, he might have rebounded and possibly we all would have had a better life. I wouldn't have derailed, and I possibly would have achieved greater heights.

Perhaps he was ahead of his time, perhaps he desperately wanted to escape the monotony of village life, but he couldn't due to various short comings and sentiments that kept people in their villages; He never wanted me in that situation and that's why he made sure I was sent away so early, despite the pain and struggle.

My mother tried her best to convince my father to move elsewhere like some of the other entrepreneurial farmers that bought property in the upland area, but he wouldn't. He was also very proud and a socially oriented person; he did not want to default on his debt and get caught in the dangerous cycle of failed businesses and bankruptcy. He refused to consider that and instead chose to pay off his debt by selling land. He ignored the disagreements about the high interest rates, without resorting to any back door practices. He wasn't bashful about asking Krishna uncle to take responsibility for my upbringing either.

His goals were clear, and he picked the right person, knowing how sincere my uncle was in keeping his word. Many young people were sent to the city to stay with their family for school. What was different about my situation was the age at which I was sent away— I was very young. He felt it was worthwhile to break that cycle of village life and that it had to be done early. He did not want me with one foot in the village and the other in the city.

As much as he sacrificed for me, he also hindered my chances by letting me down midway and leaving me to navigate things on my own. Given his impact on me and how much I adored him, everyone would have been better off if he were still around. I would have liked a failed father rather than no father, preferred his wisdom over his absence.

While we were at work, my mother spent her time knitting, calling her family in India and on long walks with Devil. She loved the dog, and we would tease her that she already had a grandson anytime she felt the need to pressure us for children. We drove around visiting nearby touristy places. She enjoyed spending time with our friends and inviting everyone over for what seemed like never-ending festivities. Meena and I loved having her with us.

When we went out to malls and parks, with her dressed in a traditional Indian sari, she always got attention, people smiled at her or approached us complimenting her on the outfit. She was thrilled to hear such compliments and gladly showed off. After Meena and I had married, my mother had gradually grown closer to my mother-in-law, developing a sisterly bond, having shared stories, situations, and experiences. When my mother-in-law passed away, upon my request, my mother postponed her U.S. travel plans and went to stay in Hyderabad to help my father-in-law during the first six months, supporting him through his grief, helping him as needed. Meena developed a deep affection for my mother, and she could relate to Meena's grief, doing her best to be her surrogate mother, caring for Meena as she would her own daughters. My mother always insisted on Meena having a good relationship with Radha.

The entire family got together towards the end of her visit in September 2001, my sisters, their spouses, and little Maya, as well as Sarat and Radha all came to visit. The same family that struggled through every step of the way for eighteen years since my father's death, now came together with a real sense of accomplishment, relief, and satisfaction.

Krishna uncle's wish to visit the U.S. remained unfulfilled because he could never get a visa, a disappointment for both of us. As much as I had disagreed with his strict, tough-love approach during my early years, over time I developed a deep respect for him, his family, and for everything they did for me. I supported uncle financially during the later phase of his life although he never accepted anything from me easily. His one request was that I support his grandchildren in their U.S. emigration efforts, which I wholeheartedly did. Most of the misery I felt during those years somehow turned into funny anecdotes that we now joke about during family gatherings.

On September 11, 2001, the senseless act of terror changed the nation. I feared that our life in the U.S. would never be the same. Until then, I'd found Americans to be the most welcoming, fun-loving, kind, practical, forgiving people you could ever meet; a land of immigrants where opportunities were handed to the best, no matter where they come from. But after 9/11, I felt threatened.

Religion, country of origin, skin tone, and any such obvious differences from "real Americans" mattered more now, going beyond the historical domestic race relations, and like what I had seen growing up in India. As much as India is a peace-loving, multi-religious, secular country, social, ethnic, and religious differences are carefully noted in every facet of one's life there and unfortunately discriminatory practices remain. Now America was becoming more inward-looking, less tolerant, less welcoming. It put immigrants and even natural-born citizens on edge.

Over the years I became close to my dear boss, Fred. He assumed the role of surrogate father and called me his third son. Even he asked me one day if I was Muslim. People in America got curious about foreigners like me, wanting to know more about them, their way of living, their religious beliefs, their experiences.

When people would ask about my religion, I tried to snuff out any reason for further curiosity, and told them about my Catholic convent school, and my childhood exposure to Christianity. That response generally seemed to placate most people. When probed a little further, I'd add that I wasn't Muslim, but some of my closest friends were, and I also knew many Hindus and Christians. Initially telling people I was born a Hindu they thought I was talking about the Hindi language. Clearly many did not know the difference between the Hinduism religion and the Hindi language. From an emotional standpoint if a non-practicing person like me could be bothered by such comments and lack of information, I can only imagine how actual practitioners must feel.

My dreams for an MBA never faded. I imagined in some sort of distorted way that if I went to Harvard, I could regain my academic glory and resurrect my past sense of opportunity. But the risk-taker in me had somehow gotten more cautious and I was unwilling to shake-up my happy, well-oiled, and seemingly rewarding life too much. So, I went to Duke University for my MBA.

They had many full-time programs that allowed working professionals to pursue an MBA and continue working. Economically and professionally, this made a lot of sense to me. Duke's reputation was excellent with near Ivy League status, making it a highly sought-after program. I kept reminding Fred of my desire to pursue the degree every chance I got.

The company eventually subsidized everything. I was incredibly fortunate that my family supported me throughout my education. Occasionally when listening to colleagues in the U.S. talk about the value of a college education was surprising to me.

I heard things like, "I can't wait for my kids to leave the house." "They are on their own paying for college." "Why would I pay?" These were educated, middle-income parents that could seemingly afford to pay. They would go on vacations or buy luxury items, things that quickly lose value, while leaving their child saddled with loans for years.

I am all for encouraging independence and responsibility for children as early as possible, and I would never advocate parents take unnecessary burdens, but to adopt such a selfish attitude toward education does them a disservice. While Indian families have a way of putting their lives on hold to support their next generation's aspirations, that initial support from the family is repaid by the children in many ways, bringing Indian families together.

The practice of living in multi-generational households is a significant cultural difference between India and the U.S. While physically residing in the same home may not always be perfect for many or done out of economic need, there are emotional and mental benefits that are perhaps lost to western families. The joy of grandparents and grandchildren being together or nearby is a natural opportunity for learning and sharing the prior generation's experience, and the younger generation's enthusiasm.

Being an immigrant who grew up with that sense of closeness, choosing to sacrifice that bond and having to shed one's past in search of a future has been one of the most excruciating parts of life. Resignation to a life with a certain type of loneliness, subconsciously lost in nostalgic memories, is a part of an immigrant's life. After my mother's first visit in 2001, we knew we wanted her to stay for extended periods, so we had to get a place to live that could accommodate that wonderful responsibility.

We sold *Maitri I*, our beloved first home, with a "For Sale by Owner" sign, giving ourselves thirty days to test my marketing skills and save a broker's fee. A neighbor a few blocks away purchased the house in cash for his son. When we moved into *Maitri II* in the city of Charlotte in December 2002 one main criteria was a bedroom for my mother on the ground level.

I started my MBA and motivated by how impressed I was with the program, Meena joined the same program, a year behind me. When my mother visited us on her second trip in 2003, the entire family came together at our home and spent four wonderful days over the Christmas break.

In 2003 Radha had a girl, Manu, who she named after her mother. While their mother's death pushed Meena and Radha apart, our conscious efforts over the prior years along with Manu's birth brought our families together. Our on-again, off-again relationship went on well for a while only to lapse again a year later when Meena's father visited the U.S. and did not visit us at all, instead staying at Radha's for several weeks.

When Radha chose to share selective details about that, it added another issue in Meena and Radha's relationship. Each time these emotions flared up and Meena confronted Radha about her choices, unwilling to escalate matters further, Radha would apologize. We would decide to accept and move on. But it was as though the relationship was always one step away from rocky terrain, just waiting for the next excuse or reason to veer off the path.

In early 2005 Sasi had a baby girl, Anjali, and my mother visited us a third time, staying with Sasi during that trip, given that Meena and I were in the middle of our MBA's. Unfortunately, for eighteen months we saw very little of each other until we finished in late 2005.

To celebrate I jumped out of an airplane from 15,000 feet! Letting go of the plane and jumping out into the sky was perhaps the most exhilarating experience of my life. Those few seconds of adrenaline is something to be experienced.

Meena and I both got promoted at our jobs as well. We had been hyper-focused on our careers and couldn't have asked for more support from our employers, friends, and family. It was a short-lived, but very rewarding and dynamic phase of our lives, despite its demanding pace.

.     .     .

## SAVING THE BEST FOR THE LAST
## JANUARY 2005

By the beginning of the twenty-first century India was increasingly part of the new global economy, adopting more *laissez faire* economic pro-investment policies. My home state of Andhra Pradesh led the nation along this new path. Many new economic opportunities were created. Hyderabad exploded in growth with thirteen million people by 2020, a far cry from the two million when I went there in 1975. As a result of all this change, in a short time my original target of $300,000 did not mean as much and was worth a lot less.

Because of globalization, IT advances, social media, and consumerism, the U.S. and its perceived way of life became even more attractive to many Indians. Some members of my extended family did quite well economically. At the same time requests for financial help from others that had not benefited started just months after I arrived. I was happy to fulfill these requests thinking of it as a good way to pay it forward by helping family, especially if it was for education, medical reasons, marriage, a small investment, or some unexpected household emergency.

Sometimes, I think I let myself get taken advantage of by some folks in India who needed money. One extreme case was a relative who convinced me to lend him a great deal of money so he could invest in his business. Four years later when I tried to call in the loan, showing an ugly side, he refused. When I insisted, he threatened to kill himself rather than sell his assets to pay his debt. Unwilling to continue to be involved with a deceitful and obviously unhealthy individual, I chose to let it go and forget the loan. That too was a lesson worth learning. I felt like some of the moral and ethical values in India have gradually deteriorated, but of course my memories could be tainted by the passage of time and the reality of distance.

In the few years we had been away from India, we realized how our perspectives on life were changing. On each of our visits to India it began to feel too hectic, too demanding, and too full of painful memories. In some ways it was the very culture itself: the ceremonial pomp, the concern about prestige and overly image-conscious values. These priorities seemed convoluted. Having been distant, we could see things we couldn't when we lived there. That's when we knew our home might no longer be in India.

Combined with Meena's reluctance to move back, Radha and my sisters comfortably settling down in the U.S. and Canada, the writing was on the wall. Perhaps we had become the very thing I promised I would never be, the people that don't return, the ones who leave a distinct past behind and start a new set of our own traditions and values. As clichéd as it may sound, after moving around the world I learned the truth of the adage, "home is where the heart is." Our past was in India, a piece of our nostalgic selves remains there. But we both realized our future was in the U.S.

Towards the end of her MBA program, a course required Meena to travel to Europe. Taking advantage of the opportunity, she and four friends, decided to visit Prague on an overnight train. When they reached the platform around 9 pm, there was a worn out, freight-train-looking-boxcar-like thing, waiting for them. Apparently, it was only the Western European trains that were high-speed. This one was going east, and was a lot like the trains in India, just a bit cleaner.

Two hours into the trip, the train suddenly stopped and then there was a knock on their door, and they heard a voice saying, "Passport check." All of them handed their passports to the officer. After a few minutes another officer who spoke a little English was brought in. He told Meena that she needed an additional visa. She was the only Green Card holder in the group, but an Indian passport. The others were U.S. citizens, without any visa restrictions even in that part of Europe. But with an Indian passport, Meena needed a visa everywhere she went. She was asked to step off the train in the pitch dark, onto the dimly lit, Cold War era platform at the border between

Hungary and Slovakia. They were instructed to stay at an inn for the night and take the return train to Budapest at 8 am the next morning.

After that horrible experience, we decided it was time to expedite our U.S. citizenship. We had qualified for citizenship earlier, but kept putting it off, unsure if we wanted to take that big step. Even though we were living in the U.S., we were reluctant to give up Indian citizenship and the passport, feeling it was our connection to home. It was a physical manifestation of our inner selves that made us feel Indian.

.        .        .

## A PROUD CITIZEN
## SUMMER 2005

The day we were sworn in as U.S. citizens was one of the happiest of my life. That I'll always be a "Naturalized alien" is obvious from my appearance. I was glad to at least shed the internal feeling of being an "alien" from then on. I hated being referred to as an "alien," even on immigration forms.

In the various forms I had to fill out, "Indian" or "Asian Indian" was not listed under the race or origin classification. Growing up in India, it was drilled into you how great your ancient heritage was, how renowned your culture is, and how much it means to world civilization; but here I was filling the forms in a 200-year-old new country, and there was no box saying Indian to check. It was like I did not really exist, that I did not matter. The only box I saw that came close was Asian. But I am not Asian. I was told when I first ticked that box that was for people of Chinese, Korean and Japanese origin.

I started filling the box marked "Other," which made me feel even less significant. For a while, I seriously considered if I was meant to be the American Indian, having missed the idiomatic difference between that and Indian American. For as far as the U.S. has come dealing with complex issues of race, ethnicity and gender, there is still work to be done. If everyone else wasn't called European-American, why were some African-American or Asian-American? I never understood.

Just as a white person in the U.S. may never ever know what being classified, viewed, and regarded a minority feels like, I didn't until I moved to the U.S. Coming here from a foreign country gave me the unique experience of being a majority and a minority in one life. I developed a new level of respect and understanding towards those having to deal with the indignity of being a minority by birth in the wrong country—at least mine was by choice. Perhaps, I thought, it is time to start living without such classifications at all?

The question "Where are you from?" has been a most interesting one over the years. Growing up in India where such questions were continuously raised due to all the ingrained characteristics within that society made it a little long winded in India. I had to explain my identity starting at the core, the family name, then language, faith, caste, village, district, region, or state orientation. After arriving in the U.S. none of that mattered, and my identity was simply that of the birth nation, my "race," requiring me to explain, "I'm from India," no matter how long I have lived here or which passport I carry.

A few years after becoming a U.S. citizen I had to answer the same question back in India, explaining that I was from India, but the locals treat you differently, identifying you more as American. When I started introducing myself saying "I'm from America," after finally accepting that I was being seen as an American, most of my international colleagues looked at me funny. It seems I don't belong anywhere. But as far as am concerned I am just an Indian in America.

Even with the best of intentions, a lot of what's possible environmentally and structurally in the U.S. is simply not possible yet in India. America is a new country in some ways, with large areas sparsely populated, giving the impression of newness, a place where people came to start over and get a new life.

India in contrast seems a weary country, a crowded landscape with myriad old customs that have remained in place over centuries, giving it a rich culture and a unique wisdom but an entrenched resistance to change. Many of those same traditions also make India too inward-looking, holding back true creative enterprising and individual expression for much of its youth.

In the U.S. with abundant social, educational, and professional opportunities, I have never seen so much available intellectual capital in every known technical, financial, medical, or scientific field. In my experience no other country has pursued capitalist endeavors with such determined passion. Retaining our early lessons from India and internalizing an American outlook, Meena and I developed our own vision of what we wanted out of life. Viewing it through our lens made us stronger personally and professionally and better people than we would otherwise have been.

We bought a new house, *Maitri III*, a waterfront home on the region's busiest sporting lake, north of Charlotte. For someone who remembers having only a few sets of clothes and shoes as a child, combined with the frugal millionaire habits I had been following, it was a new thing to want a fairly large speed boat. It did sort of feel good, but at the same time I was uncomfortable feeling like I was putting wealth on display. Maybe it was some vaguely remembered impression of the modern conveniences the wealthier men in my village had owned.

I went ahead anyway and bought the boat, and practically lived on it during good weather. But the most important item in our house was my mother's rosewood bed set, my favorite family heirloom. We had my mother send us the entire set from India soon after moving in. She was very pleased that I wanted it for my home.

Over a six-year period since her first visit in 2001, my mother shuttled between the U.S. and Canada, spending more than half her time away from India. Radha had a second girl, Ritu. Sasi's baby girl, Anjali, in Michigan and Deepa's daughter, Maya, in Ontario were growing up fast. My mother felt it was necessary to be with them and help them while their daughters were so young. I reluctantly accepted, though I wished to see more of her myself, spending time with us.

As busy as Meena and I were with our MBA's and our career aspirations, my mother felt we couldn't spare time. If she were to visit, she would be a distraction. I was torn between these choices. It always felt I was forced to save the best for the last, and I convinced myself that it was okay.

Once everything was settled after our MBA graduations and everyone was back to their normal routines, for the first time my mother said she wanted to live at our home in the U.S. permanently and visit India only as required. Also, her social circle was beginning to slowly shrink in India. Rao Tatha and Raja Babai had passed away recently, and so we planned on applying for a U.S. Green Card for her. Like anyone looking back at their life, had I known what awaited in the future I would have never wasted, what I now know to have been, some of the most important years of my life. I felt I lost precious time and had created excuses not to spend time with my family on what I thought were more important things.

# PART IV

## ENDING THE END AND STARTING THE NEW

*Death is as sure for that which is born*
*As birth is for that which is dead*
*Therefore, grieve not for what is inevitable.*

*– The Gita*

# 10

## Feeling The Unfeelable

**THAT DAY**
**MARCH 11, 2007**

I WOKE UP ON A PLEASANT Sunday morning, it was warm for that time of year. My wife was by my side, a speed boat was at the dock, an inviting lake view from the bedroom with sailboats and jet skis zipping around the water. I sighed deeply, somehow unable to appreciate the moment. Unlike our earlier times, most conversations with Meena veered into business talk, or an invariable rant about my insatiable dreams. This conversation as well wasn't the light-hearted casual talk she preferred about our upcoming trip to Italy.

I went on digging deeper into the past, remembering every little detail of what we endured, how hard things had been since childhood, talking about my ambitions, that I was meant to achieve more, and not meant to slow down. I was agonizing over my personal potential and what else I could be doing to get ahead when chance once again played a hand. It dealt an earth-shattering blow that in a few agonizing moments changed everything.

Often, I wondered how Meena could be so patient with me because I knew I could dominate a conversation and steer it my way. She'd heard me speak about my never-ending plans a million times before, yet she always found ways to encourage me and caution me at the same time. She was my biggest cheerleader and coach. What was the source of my restlessness? Is it the dream that kept haunting me, the lone warrior searching for his kingdom? Was I chasing wealth, power, or fame?

I kept arguing with Meena until she suggested that we should get out and enjoy the weather, get some fresh air. We decided to go to the new bakery for coffee and cake. As we pulled out of the driveway to head back home an unknown international number, came up on my phone I answered not knowing what it could be about. I was already stressed and nursing a bad headache. I guess the international caller ID set me off a little, a chill passed through my body as I straightened up, alerted, intently listening, as the person on the other end of the line verified my identity and introduced himself.

"Sir, we are calling you from the Ontario Police Department. I am afraid there has been a terrible road accident. It may involve someone you know."

"What?" I shrieked, my voice shaking.

"We airlifted a thirty-three-year-old woman, Deepa, a nine-year-old girl, and an older lady in a sari to the Hamilton General Hospital. They were driving a red-colored, late model, Toyota Corolla."

I could not wholly fathom what I was hearing. Deepa, Maya, my mother?

I started stuttering. "Officer ... that seems to match my family, my sister, her daughter, and my mother ... What do you mean there was an accident? What happened? How are they doing?"

"They were crossing an unguarded railway track when a freight train crashed into them. It was a severe accident; the vehicle flipped multiple times before landing upside down in a ditch 150 feet away. It took the emergency crew an hour to pry open the doors and rescue the passengers. Head injuries, chest injuries, multiple fractures possibly. I am sorry, sir.

"We found the ID on the younger lady. We could not ID the older lady. But we assumed they were related. From the cell phone we located at the accident scene, we tracked down a number they last called about thirty minutes before the accident; that person gave us your contact number as the closest family."

I wanted to cry; it struck me that at that moment for some reason I could not remember when I had last cried. But I was starting to go into some mental and emotional shut down, unable to regulate the growing fear over what was coming. I'd been in the same emotional place before when I was a boy when my father killed himself and for a moment, I was that small boy again. For once, I thought of God, desperately hoping a higher power would somehow answer my call for help. I felt lost.

"Officer, we will arrange to leave as soon as possible. We live in Charlotte, North Carolina." After exchanging further details, I hung up the phone and called Sasi in Michigan, my hands shaking. My heart was palpitating, and I had difficulty breathing. As soon as she heard my voice she broke down, wailing. "Anna[11], why should this happen to us, why again? This is so cruel!"

I have never been able to shake the feeling of impending catastrophe that lurked in the back of my mind and here it was blowing up in my face. I was shocked and disassociated enough to be able to get through the next few days. Suddenly there were a thousand painful things I would have to manage and not fall apart at the same time. Honestly if not for Meena I would not have made it.

I did my best to console Sasi. I tried to be strong, concerned that if I broke down, she would lose hope, and it would make things much worse. She always looked to me for strength. After finishing that call, I placed a couple of other quick calls, alerting friends in Charlotte, and a few others in the Toronto area about the situation, requesting their help, giving them our whereabouts and travel plans.

Mohan was abroad in Italy on a business visit, he was notified about the situation and planned to rush back as quickly as he could.

---

[11] *Anna*, means elder brother in Telugu

Meena and I stuffed necessities into a small suitcase, making sure we grabbed both our passports and hurried to the airport. My neighbor offered to take care of Devil.

I realized that I was facing something that I had always feared but had not been able to fully identify. I could be having my mother taken away again, and just after restoring a deep and important emotional connection with her. My dear mother always worried about her beloved son, the apple of her eye.

I began to realize that the bonds of blood and a spiritual connection had been strengthened by the pain from the long stretches of separation. We were just getting to know each other when my mother had decided to come live with us. I was feeling her motherly warmth for the first time, all for me. I'd waited thirty-five years for it. My mother's voice from her last call replayed over and over in my mind. She'd called from Canada the prior Wednesday, after arriving recently from a brief visit to India. We talked about her trip, her journey back, her health, and about ten minutes into the conversation, I got a call from work. I checked who it was, someone wanting to discuss some urgent manufacturing problems.

"Amma, I have someone waiting for me. Can I call you right back?"

"Sure, baabu, take care of yourself," Mother said, hiding the disappointment in her voice, wanting to keep talking to me, but unwilling to hold me back from other pressing matters. She always called me baabu, beloved son in Telugu.

"Ok, Amma. Speak soon." I hung up without thinking about it, as though another moment of my time couldn't be wasted. Had I known what was going to happen, I would have never hung up the phone. Had I realized, I would have made every attempt to call her back as promised. But of course, life never works like that. I have learned, painful as it is, regrets are only in and for the past, we need to be as mindful of our present as possible. One cannot go back and get it right on a second try.

Meena and I boarded the flight, trying our best to contain our grief, not ready to face what awaited us there. I kept seeing flashes of my mother, Deepa, Maya, their smiling faces, through my teary eyes.

. . .

## BROKEN PATH
## MARCH 12, 2007

As the plane landed at the Toronto Pearson International Airport, I turned on my cell phone and of course there were several messages from friends and acquaintances about the accident, offering help. In this moment of deep despair and fear I was comforted to know that I had a strong circle of friends and family who were willing to step up and help if asked. It was 6:30 pm in the evening, and one of Mohan's friends came to pick us up at the airport. We rushed straight to the hospital, anxious to get a medical update. Everything was a blur.

The hospital staff prepared to bring us to the sixth floor. They told us that Deepa and Mother were in the Intensive Care Unit, both in a coma. Nine-year-old Maya had died in the ambulance on the way to the hospital.

I gasped, my knees buckled, my lips trembling, and my voice choked. Unable to say a word I stared out the window, trying to fight back tears, remembering all the good times we'd spent with my niece just two months earlier over the Christmas holidays. Maya was an articulate and intelligent girl with a lovable personality and maturity beyond her age. We'd played Uno and board games, having great fun every time. She was thrilled when she unwrapped the roller skates she'd gotten at Christmas. I could not fathom how her parents were going to take this.

As I entered the attending physician's office, he got up and greeted me with a tight, reassuring squeeze of my hand, gesturing to take a seat. "I am sorry about your situation. Both your mother and sister are in critical condition. They were airlifted here seven hours ago directly to the hospital. Your sister suffered multiple chest and spine injuries, with damage to her lower neck. She is in a deep coma as of now and going through further testing. Your mother did not suffer any significant external body injuries. Still, she has severe internal brain injuries towards the back of her head. We are awaiting further tests from our brain trauma specialists as well."

I was not sure what to say, what to ask, what did all that mean? Deepa had suffered critical body damage while my mother suffered critical brain damage. Are both at risk? How critical is critical? Does critical mean fatal? "Can I see them now?" was all I could come up with in my state.

I could feel my heart pounding, my entire body trembling. We walked a few doors down to the ICU. I took a few steps and leaned against the wall, trying to compose myself. Meena, beside me, reached for my hand.

"I am fine. Let's go," I said, taking a deep breath. Inside the ICU were several rooms. It was quiet. All you could hear was the hum of the air conditioner and medical equipment beeping and pinging. As I pulled aside the thin curtain in front of the door, I saw my beloved mother and sister lying in their hospital beds, motionless. They were in medical gowns, with ventilators, tubes, pipes, wires everywhere connected to various equipment for heart, brain, other vital organ monitoring. Mother was on the bed to the left, Deepa to the right.

I turned my gaze to my mother first, taking a few steps closer until my knee touched the side of her bed, leaning into her. She was right there, yet so far away. There was silence everywhere. She was breathing softly with the ventilator, but somehow, I could feel her heartbeat. I could see the glow on her face, the same glow she always had. It just seemed like she was in a deep sleep. There was no visible injury on her face or her body, not a bruise or single cut anywhere. I held her hand gently, trying to get a response, I called her name. But she was motionless, the only sign of life being her faint breath, her fingers were unresponsive. With tears welling up in my eyes, I turned my head towards Deepa on the other bed.

Deepa was bandaged head to toe, there was not a spot on her body that was not somehow covered by some sort of clinical dressing. She had a large laceration from the left side of her mouth to the ear. Her body lay motionless from the injuries to her lung and chest, a broken collar bone, multiple fractures in the upper and lower spine, and a shattered left leg. She had taken the direct hit from the train with the most damage on her side of the car.

It felt hopeless even to try and reach closer to her, the way she was secured to keep her from moving, even though she was in a coma. Nevertheless, I leaned in towards her, slowly murmuring, "God, please do not take these people away from me."

I wished for a chance to say all that was deep in my heart. I wanted more time with my mother and sister, to make up for everything missed in my childhood to add more memories to our lives. Even more devastating was having to go to the morgue to identify my niece.

It was uncomfortably cold and not as well-lit as one might expect. Maya was lying peacefully on a table behind a large window. The surroundings were completely antiseptic, and she was covered up to her neck in a white hospital sheet, which triggered a memory of my father's dead body after his suicide. She had suffered a severe head injury that was devastating and impossible to survive. I grieved silently.

The family went back to the large waiting room upstairs, which the hospital had reserved for our large group of visitors who had gathered by then. Within a couple of hours, Sasi and Venu arrived from Michigan, and later Radha from Virginia. Seeing me, Sasi could not contain her sorrow. Both of us hugged and held each other, weeping. I escorted her back to the ICU unit, holding her hand, unwilling to let go.

By that evening, the surgeons moved my mother to the brain trauma center and Deepa was moved into another area within the ICU and began preparing her for critical surgery on her neck and spine.

The next morning there were signs of swelling on my mother's brain, so she was taken into surgery which lasted through till the late afternoon. The suspense and anxiety were oppressive. Everyone was on edge trying to do their best to put on a brave face and be supportive. The lead surgeon asked for a meeting with the immediate family. I went in with Meena, Sasi, and Venu. His prognosis of their conditions was not encouraging. He said they were doing everything they could, but that both were in critical condition. His recommendation was to keep monitoring the situation but make sure we realize the very real possibility of negative outcomes.

I kept going to my mother's room as often as I could to stay alone with her. I would sit by the side of the bed and stare at her face, thinking about her sweetness, her life, her hardships, so many emotional memories that tears were rolling down my face. She had reached a time in her life when she had finally been relieved of the troubles and burdens she had borne for so long. The difficulty of taking care of her three children, especially after my father's death, who she sacrificed everything for, as well as trying to run the family farm.

"When it is my time to go," she had always said, "I want to go quickly with as little pain and suffering as possible. I do not want to be a burden to anyone with some prolonged sickness or illness."

By the second night, Mohan was back from Italy. His grief cannot be put into words. Seeing him in that condition was excruciating for me. The following day after a short, closed casket ceremony attended by family we cremated my young niece. The whole family was there along with some of her friends and teachers from her school.

Four days later, the neurosurgeon, together with multiple specialists and the head of the hospital's neurology department, determined that my mother was not progressing, in fact she was brain dead. The chances of her recovery were little to none. We were told that "Even if she were to physically recover, she would not be who you know as your mother." Her heart was beating, but her brain was dead. I wasn't prepared to accept it. They were asking for my permission to end her life.

I imagine this is the most difficult decision a person can be faced with. The hardest choices my mother ever made in her life were about me and my well-being, and now I was faced with an even harder one. I left the room without responding. My head was pounding.

The next twenty-four hours pushed me to the limits of my ability to cope. I did not want to have to make the decision to give the medical team the permission they needed. It occurred to me at the time that it was easier to face one's own death than that of a loved one.

As I laid down on the small sofa at the corner of the waiting room early the next morning, I prayed. I prayed for strength and resolve. I prayed for courage. I prayed for forgiveness. I prayed for love. Cramming my head into the pillow, my heart seemed to fracture and again I was overcome by tears that had been held back over the previous six days. Around 7 am the next day we got everyone together to discuss what we should do next. Someone suggested that we should consider donating mother's organs. Instantly, I latched onto that idea.

"I agree. Let's do something that will keep Mother alive in spirit. Let's donate her heart and her eyes to someone that needs them. Let's celebrate her life by giving life to someone in turn, rather than letting it end so abruptly. She would have wanted this," I said, still struggling to maintain some composure. The entire family agreed it was a good idea. By the end of the morning the family members and close friends had paid their respects. Sasi and Meena read Mother's favorite scripture to her.

I went in last by myself, after everyone else had left the room. I lay quietly next to her on the bed, holding her hand, just as I did when I was a little boy, hugging her, unwilling to let her go. I cried, asking for her forgiveness. I got lost remembering all the good times we had over the years. As these memories raced through my mind. I lay next to her for a long time, hoping she might show some small sign of life, a flicker of an eyelid or move a finger. I was fearing for my own future loneliness because of her absence.

My mother had given me a wool blanket when I was young child and I first left for Hyderabad. Clinging to that blanket was my substitute for hugging my mother. Anytime I missed her I would wrap myself in the blanket. Over the years it began to disintegrate, and Satya auntie kept asking me to get rid of it, but I loved it and would not give it up. I did not part with it until I turned 17 and left Hyderabad for college.

For someone who couldn't even part with her old blanket, the hugeness of this loss was heretofore unimaginable. It was as if all the pain and deep need for connection I had experienced my whole life, was being compressed into one excruciatingly painful, infinitely small moment of intense emotion.

Finally, as I got up to leave, I gently picked up her motionless hand and placed it over my head seeking her blessings for the one last time I could physically touch her and feel her. "Thank you for everything, Amma," I said, giving her a gentle farewell kiss, choking back my tears, unable to say goodbye, while she lay there peacefully, as though in a deep sleep.

My mother had so many dreams of her own and was looking forward to our new lives together as a family in the U.S. It was hard to see her cheated out of those experiences. That made letting her go even more difficult. Finally, I walked out of the room and informed the doctor we were ready. It was only a matter of hours, after she was disconnected from all life support, she passed away peacefully. She was only fifty-seven.

All her life, my mother only knew how to give. It felt as though she decided her time was up, she had a good life on earth, and now that her three children were settled and leading comfortable and happy lives. Even in death, she gave life to seven strangers. The thought of her vital organs being helpful to someone and keeping them alive makes me pleased to think that is some very real way she lives on. At times, I desperately wish to know the identity of the person that had her heart, so I can give them a long warm hug and feel her heart beating one more time.

The next day, I performed the last rites and cremated her mortal remains at a local funeral home, in a place she had only been visiting, far away from where she belonged. Fred, my boss flew from Charlotte to attend the funeral, along with several of my cousins, family friends and other relatives. Her ashes were held in an urn to be spread on my father's land where his remains lay.

It was the most challenging day of my life. When my father passed away, I was still a child, and the situation's appalling and confusing nature overshadowed the pain. But the manner of my mother's death, knowing how her heart was still intact, every ritual I performed made me feel like I was seeking forgiveness for my helplessness and failure to save her. I'd failed to protect my mother; I'd failed to keep my promise to my father. With the loss of a parent a part of you is lost too. A part of me died with my mother that day. Every plan of ours, everything I dreamt of for my family, bringing it all together in the U.S. were suddenly wiped out. My sister was in a coma, there were two untimely deaths, and the rest of us were lost in the abysmal darkness.

Deepa remained in a deep, death-like coma for over a month, quietly fighting for her life. Following several lengthy medical procedures, she slowly started improving. Leaving her in her husband's care, supported by some family friends in Canada, the rest of us went to India with my mother's ashes.

Visiting the farm with my mother's remains brought back memories of my father and my last visit there years earlier burying the money he gave me. I was at the exact spot to give that land the final remains of my beloved mother, to share a part of her with the dirt signifying our ancestral roots, the place where life meant for my father and mother to be together again, now forever.

After returning from India, with the help of the local press in Toronto, we lobbied the Canadian authorities to install a railroad crossing arm at the site of the accident. The publicity surrounding the accident was instrumental in helping with this lobbying effort. I offered to pay for installation to ensure that at least this would be the last time an accident would happen there. Given the enormous support we received through the press and the public, the local authorities decided to allocate sufficient funding towards the required changes to improve that crossing, including installing crossing gates.

Even with all the advanced medical care available at the Toronto hospital, it took Deepa over a year to be able to function independently, and two years to get back to her normal self, enabled by patient, superhuman, loving care from her husband. I have seen and read about many marriages that did not survive such catastrophes. But somehow, he overcame his grief and the loss of his daughter to care for Deepa. My respect and regard for Mohan grew to a deep admiration for his courage, positivity, and love of life. He is a great husband. As I was struggling with the immediacy of my pain, I felt that what we wish for, what we settle for, where we start and where we end up, nothing seemed to be in our control.

•     •     •

## FAMILY OF MY DREAMS
## MAY 2007

There was an outpouring of support from my friends and colleagues in the U.S. and all my family in India. But I wasn't ready to accept sympathy from anyone. I was ashamed of myself; I felt like I'd failed at everything, and my dreams were shattered. Even though I knew rationally it was something beyond my control, I still felt like I'd been unable to protect my family and care for them.

Since my father's death, I had decided, deep down, that my life's purpose was to care for my family and improve our situation. But at that point it felt like my purpose had been lost. It felt like everything that had been accomplished up until that point had been for nothing. As imperfect as this country is, until then I felt it had been perfect for my family, but now I felt it also had its drawbacks. Our lives were deficient because of how it divided us and spread us apart, sacrificing family ties and emotional bonds.

I questioned everything we had done. Neither of my two sisters had originally wanted to be in the U.S. nor had Radha. They would have been content living in India, marrying, settling down like many others. But I nudged them, pushed them, encouraged them, opened a path towards a different life in America. In my mind I wanted them to experience everything Meena and I had planned for ourselves.

Since my childhood, one thing I was always confident about, as was everyone else around me, was that I had a knack for figuring things out and often turning difficulty into opportunity. No one ever doubted in my ability to do well professionally, in fact it was expected. Buoyed by this confidence and support while growing up, I always said I would bring everyone with me because I wanted everyone to be as successful and happy as I was. I thought that this was really the best thing we could all do. Encouraged by my example, others started to make their way forward.

What had I done, I wondered? Could I have done what I did because I subconsciously knew I was never going back to India; was that the underlying motivation for my desire to see everyone here and for everyone to be near me? Would things have been better if everyone had remained in India? Simply going back with Meena and visiting on occasion, every few years, like many other immigrants?

Unlike so many who go to work in the U.S. I did not send money to build a house for my mother, I felt guilty about this. But selfishly, I had thought that if I improved the house in India, she would not visit me as much and I wanted her to spend time with us. Would she be alive, if I had done that, I sadly wondered? I managed to encourage the generally reticent Deepa to be more outgoing and independent.

She started driving a car, learned computer programming, and secured an office job, but had it led to the accident? Wouldn't she have been better off staying in her comfort zone? *What had I done to everyone?*

I was afraid that when people looked at me, they saw an ill-fated soul whose life was somehow destined for incessant suffering. Some sort of Karmic justice, some curse from a past or present life playing its nasty hand. I was in constant emotional turmoil. One parent dead by suicide, another hit by a train, and then another hit by a bus! What did my family or I ever do in this life to deserve all this relentless grief? Could Karma be true?

Unable to find answers to these painful questions, I kept blaming myself and everything around me for all that happened. I would shy away from people and keep to myself, maintaining as much silence as I could. My usual laugh and cheerful demeanor completely vanished. I had so many dreams about my mother spending the rest of her life with us.

Just like Nanamma and Devamma, had been their family's matriarchs, I had imagined my mother being like that for our family. Living together in our beautiful lake home with my two sisters and their families nearby, Radha and many an extended family that had come to the U.S. We'd be all one happy family, coming and going, visiting each other. I kept seeing her everywhere I turned and could not bring myself to stay in that house any longer. Even the beautiful lake view from my house seemed sullied.

My mother had served as our bridge to India over the previous few years, while we made career and education the center of our lives. I was worried we would have nothing to look forward to anymore in India, that we would become isolated and gradually distanced from most things there, including my extended family. When the bridge is gone, the distance invariably grows ... no matter how near everything seemed.

Two months after the accident, I got a chance to switch my career entirely and do something different, running an e-commerce company, in a new industry that I had no expertise in. The offer was from a group with operations in the U.S. and other countries, including Hong Kong, the UK, and Germany for a leadership role as its U.S. president, in a new branch being set up in Texas. The interesting thing was, although based out of the U.S., the parent company had its roots in India.

I suddenly felt a calling. This opportunity would give me a chance to remain connected with India, give back what I'd learned in America and help develop a company with direct ties home. But given the start-up nature of that business and the disorganization of the particular e-commerce industry, we knew it was a major risk. Nevertheless, I was desperate for change both professionally and emotionally. As hard as it was to leave my German employer, I decided to accept and move on. Meena also felt a change of scenery would do us good, and that the move could help me get past my emotional and mental difficulties.

When we were in India for my mother's last rites, we had no choice but to part with everything she had at our family home, recognizing that none of us would be coming back and staying there, or needing any of it. Many things that were precious to my mother suddenly seemed worthless. That made me realize how ephemeral most of life is. Everything we seek and treasure seems so insignificant and irrelevant the minute we are gone.

Upon returning to the U.S., entirely disillusioned, and repulsed by everything materialistic, and with the new job offer, I started selling most of our worldly possessions at our lake home. This included the boat and other such toys, the furniture, the art, all things we invariably got attracted to despite my strong feelings about savvy millionaire traits. We only kept a few items that we would need for daily life. I wanted to sell the home as well. But unsure about the future risks we might be undertaking with my new job, we decided it was prudent to wait.

The one piece of furniture we kept besides the essentials was my mother's rosewood bed set. Struggling with the complex emotions bouncing around my mind, we landed in Austin, Texas, together with our dog, Devil. Meena was able to strike a deal with her company to work remotely, while I settled into my new role. We rented a townhouse, choosing a minimalistic lifestyle.

I had to cross a small railroad track on my way back and forth to work each day. The initial month or so it was difficult for me to drive across the tracks. I was still driving the same car we bought when my mother came on her first visit to the U.S. One day I sat by the crossing, unable to proceed as tears kept rolling down my cheeks. For the first time since my mother passed, I cried my heart out, wailing, banging the steering wheel, kicking the floorboard. Helpless, uncontrollable grief overtook me. I sold the car the next week. I was desperate to get rid of her memories that haunted me. I did not want anything around me reminding me of what we lost.

I suffered through bouts of grief-stricken panic attacks for the next year and a half. When it happened in front of Meena at home once or twice, she was worried about me. She'd seen the wild, angry, ambitious, creative, friendly, loving, and caring side of me, but never this vulnerable and emotional side of me. Given her struggles with her own mother's passing, she could relate to my state of mind and offered comfort.

My earlier dream of the lone warrior wandering around deep forests in search of his kingdom, which had disappeared for some years, now returned to torment me again. We led a solitary life for a year and a half, spending our time exploring Texas. Work kept me busy. It got exciting for a while, then stressful just as quickly.

The assumptions the original investors made when setting up the venture never panned out. Within six months, we started to falter. As the president of the company, it was all happening under my watch. Although my team had nothing to do with the original strategy, we felt responsible. No matter what, it wouldn't reflect well on me. Together with my team, I worked as hard and as creatively as possible to save the company.

I had left my lucrative, thirteen-year career with a multibillion-dollar international company, a place that would have continued to offer me terrific prospects over time, it now seemed like the worst move I'd ever made. But being a failure or a loser was not an option. For a while, nothing seemed to work, and the board finally decided to shut it down. But fortunately, revenues started picking up at the last minute and along with a revised business and product strategy, we saw an opportunity to save the company.

The management appreciated my efforts and asked me to take over the branch in London, UK, which was faltering. Even with Meena's career, the distance, the commute involved with this assignment, and the impracticality of it all, it still appealed to me.

By then, my overwhelming desire for a stable family returned. Devastated by our losses, we were desperate for family. Sasi and Deepa were in equal or more pain than me, and they had their own lives recover with. Radha and Sarat, living in Virginia, maintained closer ties with us following my mother's passing. Sarat's mother had sadly succumbed to an acute illness in India prior to my mother's death.

Each of us were feeling lonely and distraught from the death of important people in our lives. I felt we would all know to respect each other and see the value of family more than ever. Several of my collegemates from India had also settled in Virginia. I thought moving there would give us the benefit of being among friends. Driven by my emotions I decided that we had enough suffering and that we needed to do whatever was necessary to create a fulfilling emotional future for ourselves. Eager to have family around her young daughters, Radha latched onto this idea wholeheartedly. Sarat welcomed this decision and looked forward to us coming to live with them. Although Meena was initially reluctant, I convinced her that we all should put aside what I felt were petty disagreements and shift base to Virginia and go live with Radha and Sarat and be one happy family.

Despite all the differences no one ever doubted the admiration we had for each other. We imagined we would build a new home for all of us eventually, and Meena and Sarat would possibly start a new business. We dreamt of all four of us raising Manu and Ritu together.

We left Texas and moved to Virginia in high spirits. Meena worked from home, traveling as needed, and I was always traveling so Virginia made sense geographically as well. Leaving Meena there in fall 2008 to carry on with her work, I started commuting to the UK. The company gave me a month to figure things out. With such a short time, my only option was to cut back the company's expenses as much and as fast as possible, stabilize everything, and then attempt to grow the company.

As positive results started trickling in, the employees began to have faith in my plans. I led by example, in line with the company-wide austerity measures, by boarding myself at a cheap airport motel on Heathrow's wrong end, driving a used rusty car, worse than "8316" in India. I reduced my trips, unwilling to spend an extra penny of company funds beyond the bare minimum and chose to stay over longer periods until things stabilized. When Meena arrived to see me after my first several weeks living there, she was shocked by the overall state of affairs with the company, the hotel, the car. She questioned the viability of it all.

The business began to improve and started generating profits. Slowly, our U.S. division came back to life as well. The challenge of saving jobs, rebuilding the company, driving it towards growth and profitability gave me a huge rush. I was no longer a small cog in a big wheel. I realized the importance of good leadership. It is not power but a people centric responsibility, and I started evolving from a taskmaster to an empathetic corporate steward, fulfilling most of the professional leadership dreams of mine.

London became my base of operations. I routinely spent over 200 days a year out of the country, commuting to the UK weekly, and from there to many other parts of the world, where we had operations and supply bases. Some weeks, it was three different continents, flying to Asia for a day's meeting on occasion or hitting thirteen cities in fourteen days. The airport gate agents started greeting me by my first name, inquiring about my well-being when I had missed a flight the prior week.

We went to Virginia with great hope for our collective future, but right from the get-go it seemed that we might not be as welcome as I had hoped, as evidenced by Radha and Sarat's behavior in certain social situations. It felt they were suddenly nervous about our presence even amidst our shared social network, as though we were intruding into their safe zone. I kept ignoring things, desperate to make it work, and for a brief period I was on cloud nine. Being with Radha and Sarat, and their children, seemed perfect. It was the best thing we had done for ourselves after everything we had been through.

We quickly adapted to their daily routine, helping around the house, playing with, and caring for little Ritu, taking Manu to preschool. The high point of our stay was Devil's tenth birthday celebrations as an excuse to have a big party with about eighty people. But the warm feelings didn't last long, and slowly after the initial emotional rush wore off, we were unable to rekindle real warmth beyond happy hour type celebrations.

Things were still going okay for six months until my father-in-law's health took a turn for the worse and he died in India from a brief, rare illness during summer 2009. This crisis created a new rift between the sisters. They could not agree on how to manage things related to their father's hospitalization, death, and even the last rites, let alone the disposal of his few remaining assets.

It was clear old wounds weren't mended and everything was being done without acknowledging and addressing the root causes. Feelings buried deep inside their hearts could never be altered, no matter what, but I did not see this until that point. As was my wont I was blind to the shortcomings of those I loved. In my mind I refused to accept the reality of who people were, and instead tried to force things to go the way I thought they should go, still firmly believing that I could fix any situation and find a happy solution.

Communications started breaking down rapidly after my father-in-law's death and the relationship suffered. A few months later Meena and I began to feel insulted when Sarat did something underhanded, working against my interests in an opportunistic manner, over a key matter pertaining to a charity we had been associated with in memory of my mother, and then deliberately avoided facing me. I could clearly see their apathy towards us for the first time.

When we moved to Virginia, all of us knew we would have to deal with Radha's insecurities or Meena's frustration or my overbearing, strong will. But I had not expected my old friend and who I considered a brother to behave the way he had, and it struck me like a bolt of lightning and completely caught me off guard. I always regarded my relationships and friendships as though they were sacred. I believe that in a strong relationship there is the ability to love someone knowing each other inside out, and a friendship is the willingness to do whatever it takes to stand by someone during their moments of crisis. My inability to evoke similar warmth towards me from someone I considered a dear friend and wholeheartedly welcomed into my family felt like a personal failure. I was disillusioned that the one time I really needed him, he let me down so badly.

This felt like disloyalty; he knew how emotionally wound up I was after my mother's death, and how important what I wanted to do with this charity. It felt that of the choices he had to make, he picked the worst possible, at least from our vantage point; and Radha stood by watching, tacitly supporting. I thought I didn't matter to him, and nothing I had ever done for him mattered. I was angry and felt wronged, and I decided enough was enough. I had reached real low point emotionally.

Meena was less bothered by her disagreements with her sister and more disturbed by Sarat's attitude towards us, something we never noticed until then. Sarat or Radha making choices that would go against their own family were something Meena or I never imagined, particularly on matters pertaining to my interests. The very things that were meant to bring us together seemed to be tearing us apart right from the very beginning.

Meena and Radha's strained relationship, their mother's death, the issues with the father, the disagreements, and now the charity. Our dreams for raising the little girls together did not matter anymore. Our dream for a close bonding with Radha and Sarat did not matter. Our shared aspirations of starting a business together did not matter. Our dream to be near my other friends did not matter. Nothing that we shared could keep us together at that point. When we first arrived there, we truly adopted their home as ours and did not feel awkward about it at all. But now, the very same house didn't seem the same; it felt they did not want us there, as though they made a mistake and were stuck between us and a hard place.

That was when I realized I had lost both the family I wanted for myself and a friend in my attempts at fulfilling my desire for new life in this new world. Until then I was the glue that kept things together since my mother-in-law's passing. Until then, as much as I always knew and felt that Meena was in the right on most matters pertaining to her sister, I had encouraged her to work to patch things up with Radha, fearing for their relationship and my friendship, and hoping to save the family I wanted.

In the end it turned out there was little left to really salvage. I believed that two and two would become a four or more, but here it has slowly become a zero. A big zero. My heart broke all over, just like after my mother's death. I was worried about what people would think. I was worried for the children. I felt ashamed of not being able to realize my dream once again. But I had no intention of being antagonistic toward Radha or Sarat by remaining there and showing any animosity.

Internally stung by their behavior and recognizing that it wasn't easy having us there, I curtailed my weekly travels back to Virginia and Meena spent increasing amounts of time in London with me hoping to give everyone some space and for the situation to improve. But nothing really changed. Not only did nothing change, but there wasn't any outreach, and we were never asked about our distance and our visible discomfort. None of us seemed willing to really talk about the situation.

Any secret hope Meena and I had for a reconciliation with them never came. Bewildered and distraught I could not articulate my own nebulous feelings even to myself. But one thing I was clear about: we weren't going to beg for a dialogue no matter what, given that their thoughtless choices with disdainful indifference towards my mother's memory led to this situation. I just could not look past that. If they weren't ready to work on what was broken, we couldn't either.

After six months of this cold war drama, Meena and I decided that it was best to leave; when we told them I saw a sense of relief on their faces, and that hurt even more. While they wanted family, it was clear they weren't prepared to *be* family. They never inquired why we would leave Virginia, making an about turn, letting go of all our shared dreams from just eighteen months earlier. They never attempted to keep us there and stop us from leaving. It seemed that their insecurities took over and they simply didn't care.

Perhaps this relationship was never meant to be the way I had wanted, and it remains the biggest disappointment of my life. Unable to distance myself from the dream of the perfect family, I thought these were feelings only I could understand, feelings that meant little to anyone else, feelings that were on par with the loss of my mother. Although I knew that individually we have good marriages, I grieved the death of my dream. I was so vested in this idea of a large family, and such was my fondness for Sarat and Radha that letting go of my dream meant letting go of them as well.

I had to slowly recognize my own flaws, learn to stop overcompensating for my childhood emotional deprivation by trying to find that family everywhere around me. While with sufficient drive I had attained material success, I had to painfully realize that I could not, simply, will my way to the family of my dreams. Although I must admit, occasionally seeing other large families opened old wounds, reminding me of what I thought was my own failure, my dream was no longer the large extended family. It was more insular, mainstream, nuclear, the traditionally accepted American version: Meena, me, and whoever else life brought to us.

Since Meena had been traveling hectically with her own job by then, we felt returning to live in Charlotte, at our lake home, near to her corporate office would help cut back her trips. All the earlier desire to live in the most "happening" places vanished. Everything unappealing about Charlotte earlier disappeared after all the traveling I had done. I began to slowly realize I needed to feel like we had a stable domestic life of our own and that we should try to modulate our wishful thinking somewhat.

Although I am never one to give up so easily without fighting hard for something I truly believe in and want, this one time I did just that.

Meena and I eventually left for Charlotte dejected, but quietly without any sort of big flourish. We did it by protecting everyone's dignity, distancing ourselves from everything we truly loved, and choosing to focus on our lives rather than continue to live in a difficult and dysfunctional way. We swore to never return until we received a meaningful apology and learned to redefine our dreams of the life we imagined for ourselves, recognizing its flaws. I only realized later that expecting my vision for a family and my sense of purity towards a relationship and friendship to be unquestionably accepted by everyone else was at the root of my dissatisfaction. It was an impractical expectation.

Internally I was in a bad place, my mother's death combined with this new setback with Radha and Sarat. I felt terrible and kept blaming myself. Three years after my mother's passing, despite all the travels and business fervor, the loneliness in our lives was catching up with us more than ever before. Time can be a great healer, but it wasn't working for me. The lone warrior dreams kept haunting me. My sense of purpose was missing.

Seeing me that way also weakened the normally upbeat Meena. We did our best to get normalcy back into our lives, bonding with cousins and friends. But deep inside, nothing felt right. The gut-wrenching pain never went away. Something was missing, a gaping void. It felt like changing the course of our path would make us happier.

We started a small charity that focused on girls' education in India. Our goal was to support rural girls and women through expanding basic education, economic opportunity and strengthening the capacity for self-help to empower women to lead more independent lives and help work toward a more progressive society. It was a great cause, but I was mentally elsewhere.

# 11

## Building a Family of My Own

**A RENEWED PURPOSE**
**SPRING 2010**

I T FELT LIKE MY INTERNAL DRAMA was in its last act. Am I happy? Who am I really? Over several days in early 2010, reflecting deeply, I started going over the different parts of my life to that point, looking more deeply at my journey. Similar moments of reflection had only solidified my resolve to pursue greater material success.

What was I really striving for? Wealth, power, fame, none of these had ever been my goal, even when we had lacked so much. I never set out to change the world, cure cancer, or make it to Mars. It was always about my family. I only wished to change the fortunes of my family and those around me.

My earliest motivation was to help get my family out of grief and hardship. I was focused on helping my sisters, pleasing my mother, fulfilling my father's dream, living up to his expectations, bringing dignity to our lives, and healing the pain in everyone's heart. I never cared about money, private planes, yachts, or vacation homes. Rather, I wanted a decent life with my family, and for those near and dear to me. The professional success we achieved combined with our relatively modest lifestyle positioned us to be able to make choices.

Somewhere along the line, doing better and better got out too far ahead of me. Chasing success became a sort of addiction. Perhaps a small part of it was there from the beginning when my father sent me out into the world. Certainly, some of it was due to my father's suicide and my resolve not to fail. Whatever it was, once that demon took over, my mind was in a constant state of excitement. Something was missing. I needed to fill a void by trying to meet unarticulated expectations and working for some unknown greatness. Slowly I began to see it would be a never-ending race, with the finish line moving forward at last as fast as everything else. It would be an unquenchable fire.

As the haze started clearing, I slowly realized that success is not one-dimensional and cannot be measured as a static and unchanging set of goals. Only *I* can define what success was going to be for me. Success must not be defined only by some outside hegemonic material scale. I saw the pursuit of the tangible was substituting for the unmet needs of the emotional which had caused so much pain.

Ignoring the emotional elements without adapting renders material achievement meaningless. Carefully balancing these things, while sticking to your own path, can help determine overall happiness. The first step, for me, was to realize the need to examine my life in the first place. It took a series of serious physical, professional, and emotional setbacks that brought me to my knees to make me understand the need for balance in my life. I had been going along, but I did not really have any idea of my destination.

Success as a state of mind can make you feel good sometimes, but it should be pursued without losing sight of some real separate purpose. When my father sent me off, I spent my early life deprived of the relationships I craved, seeking solace in personal friendships and connections, but seeking success as others saw it. My father's choice to take his own life removed the blanket of security and emotional support from mine. After winning Meena's heart, I innocently got distracted from that blissful union, getting caught up in professional ambition.

Losing the opportunity to savor my mother's warmth even when I had the opportunity to potentially take part in it, made personal emotional satisfaction even more difficult. We had a large home, household furnishings, appliances, and electronics we never had in my childhood, but the one aspect that seemed to evade me was truly emotionally gratifying relationships—other than my wife. My sense of purpose was missing once again, while the difficulty and pain of separation have continued to define a large part of my life.

One of my mother's biggest wishes was for Meena and me to have children. We always found ways to gently shush her. "We don't need any other children in our lives after marrying off two girls at a young age. Their children and Radha's children are ours," we'd tell her.

She'd roll her eyes and tell us that it's never the same, "Your children are yours." We feared any additional responsibilities, and just wanted an untethered life, being under no illusions about what raising a child would be like. I was afraid of the burden of having children interfering with my professional aspirations, and concerned about failing at family life, like my father. I had lived my life as if I was meant to achieve "something", continuously proving myself, always under an enormous amount of pressure. I tried to prepare for the next bad thing, the next big contest to go on indefinitely, not as though I was simply meant to live.

Someone once told me slow down and smell the roses, but I brushed it off as something for losers, I wasn't going to slow down. There was nothing to slow down for, this is who I was. But after my mother's death my story increasingly became more directed toward mental and emotional priorities, and I started viewing life through a broader lens.

Given the emotional void created by everything that had transpired, our prior clarity on not having children didn't seem that clear any longer. We were both struggling enormously with the inner loneliness from the absence of family. Although we miss their company and the children but given the complexity of our relation and the closeness we imagined with Radha and Sarat never materialized, and unwilling to make ourselves vulnerable any longer, we thought it best to wish them well and choose to love them quietly from a distance, from our own home base. Sasi moved to Seattle and Deepa to Houston, following new professional promotions for Venu and Mohan. Having close relationships with my sisters was limited by practical obstacles. All the opportunities America offers for individual progress also pushes people to relocate, keeping families apart, adversely impacting their emotional development and stability.

One day Meena approached me, visibly upset. "I have a premonition that something else bad may happen to us in our lives. We haven't seen the end of it. If anything were to happen to me, I know you'd be lost in your life beyond redemption. And the same is true if the situation is reversed. You will be forty by the end of next year, with me right behind you. We had debated a lot about having children. At this point it is now or never. Having lost so much in our personal lives, we want something in our lives that could be our own. Having a child would bring some real joy into our days."

Meena is very balanced and thoughtful, and not one to speak in haste. With this nudge from her, it didn't take much convincing after that. Bringing in a new life to fill the gap created by those now gone seemed to be an opportunity for fulfillment by completing the circle of life. We both agreed that it would be a great way to honor my mother's memory by fulfilling the one thing she most wished for. Meena's mother would have wanted the same thing. It felt like we would be celebrating those special lives by remembering them in their grandchild, while also making us happy at the same time. My mother's words and wishes served as our beacon in our moments of darkness and added new meaning to our lives. We would have been happy either way, but we knew we deeply wanted a girl. An angelic, healthy baby commemorating the beloved mothers we lost.

.     .     .

## SEEKING BALANCE
## MARCH 2011

What turned out to be the night before the birth, we went to bed early hoping to get a good night's rest, but Meena woke me up at 11 pm, saying she was having contractions. We called the doula, and she advised Meena to relax and wait until morning. Unable to sleep we decided to head to the hospital around 5 am and Meena was admitted. We imagined the birth of our child would happen in no time, but nothing happened for several hours. All the practice sessions came in handy, and Meena stayed calm, breathing with soft meditative music.

I parked myself on a corner couch working away, taking my regularly scheduled meetings by phone, responding to all my emails. Around 2:00 pm, I got tired of waiting and went to the nearest diner to get a burger. By the time I returned, casually slurping down a tasty milkshake, Meena was in pain, the intensity of which I only realized from the evil eye I got when I innocently tried to offer her some of it, totally oblivious to the reality of her situation.

Within minutes the doctors were summoned, the soothing music was switched to rock, and the baby came kicking into this world eyes wide open to *Smells Like Teen Spirit* by Nirvana and *Sweet Emotion* by Aerosmith. Thankfully, I avoided getting verbally thrashed within an inch of my life by Meena because I had missed the arrival of our baby by sitting at the cafe a few extra minutes, lazily drinking a milkshake. After watching Meena experience the pain and joy of carrying and delivering a child, I have a huge appreciation for every woman that chooses to do it.

On that rainy day in March 2011, four years, almost to the day, after my mother and niece passed, our daughter was born. We were both ecstatic with joy, welcoming her into this fascinating world. Holding her for the first time, wrapped snugly in a tiny blanket, was one of the high points of my life. My grin couldn't have been any wider, my heart couldn't have been any fuller.

Two days later, we brought her home and took her straight to her bedroom to rest on my mother's rosewood bed. That was hers from then on, serving as her connection to her departed grandmother and other ancestors, bonding the traces of the past with the promise of the future. Only after having our child, for the first time in my life, could I feel what true love is. Unadulterated, pure, ethereal love. The kind of unconditional love poetry is all about. Loving a partner, a spouse, that first love, loving a parent, a sibling, nothing was the same as the love I had for my child.

What I saw in my mother's eyes, I could feel for myself in my heart with my child. Eight days after the birth, I started back on my travels leaving our new baby and Meena all by themselves. Meena managed on her own, juggling everything with the baby for the next few weeks until Sasi and Anjali visited for a few days, and later the nanny we hired started working to help with the baby.

We wanted time to bond with the little one during those initial days. I could not let go of the baby during my visits home. Giving her baths, playing with her and being with her as much as possible became my favorite past time. Our happiness remained inexhaustible over the following weeks. That's when we fully understood the wisdom of Mohan and Deepa's decision to have a child a year after Deepa recovered from the accident, a healthy little boy Prem, named after his deceased grandmother Prabha and sister Maya. We learned that a child could fill part of a void and give a deep sense of fulfillment to our life.

We vowed to raise this child to her full potential, with few expectations from our side and the freedom to do everything she would want to do. We would be the cool, responsible parents, giving her the best of everything we could without making her entitled. She was to be the most welcome visitor in our lives for years to come, replacing everyone gone. She was to be the guest in our abode until she could learn to fly on her own. Our role was to provide her with the necessary skills and tools required to find true north in her own life. That was our promise.

Devil passed away within a few weeks of our daughter's birth. His health had deteriorated in his final few weeks. It was as if he was in a rush to go as our surrogate child all those years while we adamantly denied the need for offspring. We never fully realized how much we had bonded with him until he was gone. It felt as though we were cursed, nothing we loved dearly could be with us for long. Engulfed with grief, I sat alone on the dock at the lake and unloaded the heaviness in my heart that evening.

"What's next, now that the baby is here?" my company asked me at one of the board meetings around that time.

"How do you feel about all the travel and your schedule?" In their infinite wisdom, they knew something more than me at that time.

"It's business as usual." I said, brushing off the question, engrossed in a spreadsheet I was reviewing. Everyone laughed at my seeming unflappability.

A couple of months later, with no prior symptoms, my back froze on me, it happened, not when I was lifting weights but while I was picking up a paper that fell off the nightstand. I collapsed, unable to move. Shortly thereafter at a lunch meeting with an investor, I slumped on the floor, due to a pinched nerve in my back and had to be taken by ambulance to the hospital. In another few weeks, my knee locked up on a treadmill and left me in intense pain for several days. My body seemed to be giving up.

I'd injured my knee and back simultaneously from a combination of running with incorrect form and travel-related stress. All that flying began to take its toll. I thought I was enjoying it and felt invincible. I ignored all the caution, imagining nothing bad would happen to me. Until then I seemed to be in the best shape of my life physically, and on top of the world professionally. But my vulnerabilities with my personal and professional lifestyle, a weakened body from all the physical and mental stress was laid bare in front of me. I was desperate for relief and traveled the world, even looking for non-traditional fixes for my back: Chinese medicine, Indian remedies, Balinese and Thai techniques, "quack" doctors—nothing worked. Was this an early warning of some kind, a sign for me to reset my mode of operation, I began to wonder?

Meena chose not to travel anymore. Any time she could spare away from her busy job, she was with the baby. While we hired a nanny for the first few years to help offload some of the physical chores, we did not want the baby to be raised by a nanny any more than needed. Meena wanted the child to get the attention she deserved from her mother. But all that was exhausting her, even with help. Respecting how much joy I sought from my career, and being a professional woman herself, she didn't insist on me adjusting any of my schedules to remain home more.

I was not home a lot of the time and I felt separated from them. That meant Meena and the baby had a routine going that I was not part of. I felt like an outsider, intruding into their world. As much as I loved spending time with the baby, I started missing my time with Meena, how we used to be earlier on, glued to each other. Now it seemed we barely had the opportunity to speak. When I told her I was upset with how our days were being spent during my limited time at home, she advised me to accept it as another reality of parenting life, which might not change much for the coming few years.

One of the interactions with my daughter that kept pushing me to consider making some real changes in my work and home life, was the iPad incident I described at the beginning of the book. I came home from a trip early and went to see my daughter and wife in the bedroom and my daughter didn't recognize me. Rather than come to me when she heard my voice, she crawled over to her iPad. I was shattered that she seemed to think that I was a small face on a screen. At that moment I felt all the weight of the stress from my job, my physical and emotional pain, and a real distance from my family. While we had a child seeking balance in our lives, it seems the balance we sought still evaded us.

Is that the price I was willing to pay? I couldn't answer. How would my daughter be, growing up with me not being around much of her early life? Would everything just get better over time? Or, just like many families, adjust, simply learn to adapt, and accept? But then I thought, aren't these two people the best things in my life? Am I saving the best for the last like I always do, by spending more time on my career first? What is it that I wanted?

We'd seen families of busy friends do just fine, regardless of the effort they put in, some even with little-to-no effort. I have seen other families torn apart, children being derailed, couples falling apart, even when they did their best to be loving and responsibly attending to every detail, cheering at all the ball games and soccer practices, going out on regular date nights. There isn't a universal solution readily available, a magic recipe that works for all. I was unhappy and combined with my new health problems, I struggled with balancing my professional aspirations with my personal desires, unsure of how to go about it.

Nevertheless, I kept going, leaving everything the way it was on the personal front, but becoming more focused professionally, like I always do when faced with a choice.

The answer came to me, as it had so often in my life, with deep introspection aided by external triggers. Fourteen years earlier, researching MBA's, I learned about a course Harvard offered called Advanced Management Program. Getting accepted was a means to professional stardom. Many participants had risen to the highest ranks of their fields. The two-month on-site program was to help expand their outlook by providing a theoretical framework for good corporate governance, focusing on senior leadership's needs.

Given my prior successes with turning around and stabilizing companies, and the genuine belief in my future potential, I felt Harvard would be instrumental in forwarding my career. All my struggles with spending much of my time away from my family, the health issues, nothing could keep me from joining the Advanced Management Program in the Spring of 2012, just thirteen months after my daughter's birth. I would only see my little girl and Meena once during those two months.

In the middle of the core curriculum, one class left a lasting impression. "How Will You Measure Your Life?" It was one lecture that discussed a set of guidelines on finding meaning, to help leaders think about innovation and growth within the structures of sound management theory. Topics like these discussed with such a group are akin to discussing environmental pollution with oil riggers. They are brushed off as fake news, a soft subject, not one meant for high achievers and heavy hitters. *Teach us how to be better bounty hunters, not better philosophers,* we thought.

The professor had a vast body of knowledge; he was a former CEO who turned a massive health crisis into a philosophic transformation.

He ingeniously flipped the topic around and asked all the business leaders the following three questions, urging them to take the remainder of their time at Harvard to find meaningful answers:

First, how can I be sure that I'll be happy in my career?

Second, how can I be sure that my relationships with my spouse and my family become an enduring source of happiness?

Third, how can I be sure I'll stay out of jail?

Similar questions had been posed to me earlier, even during my MBA program at Duke. The key takeaway for many other participants was to be good corporate stewards while thinking about the broader social impact. But somehow, this time, my reaction was entirely different. I applied it to me personally, taking it a step further, delving inside, and going as far as possible. Everything discussed struck me profoundly, leaving me thinking about it for days afterward.

.     .     .

## THE BEST COMES FIRST FROM NOW ON
## SUMMER 2012

Thanks to the sixty-day immersion program at Harvard, I got a break from the day-to-day routine of my job. It ended up being the catalyst I needed to reevaluate the path I was on. It would have been easier for me just to forget the experience, shake it off, and pretend it didn't matter. But I didn't.

The experience of my daughter not knowing who I was had never left me and the possibility of her growing up without me bonding with her I didn't take lightly. Would chasing my self-absorbed dreams with constant separation from my family driven by poorly understood ambition, risking my physical and mental health, help me help my daughter to grow up and face the world? Was it a good way for Meena to spend her time? Is that how I wanted to lead the remainder of my life, achieving some things but deliberately giving up others? My previous boss, Fred, who had since retired, did just that, traveling much of his career in high powered jobs, but then drifting away from his own family over time, which eventually lead to his divorce around age 65.

I realized Meena had gotten accustomed to my attitude and supported my dreams and desires; we tried to rationalize away what we were losing in personal time, connection, and bonding. We had almost effortlessly set aside the early promises about not separating but we got consumed by larger-than-life aspirations.

The one thing I generally lacked was a lasting father figure to guide me, coach me, and offer support when needed. In my quest to succeed, I learned most of everything I knew through chance, trial, and error, being my own judge of right and wrong, and seeking mentors wherever possible. Although Krishna uncle was one such strong figure, I could not connect with him as a father. He was never on a power trip or intended to lord over me in any malicious way. He always wanted what was best for me, and he taught me many important things, even if I would not have admitted it at the time. I agreed with his values. I could, however, never try to teach someone the way he had.

Why should I be absent as a father from my little girl's daily life, knowing how much I missed my father? Why should Meena endure my prolonged and continued absences? Most of my life I did what was expected of me, fulfilling the expectations an Indian family has of their children, stated or not, feeling a sense of burden to prove myself and be there for my family.

Here was a perfect opportunity for me to do something different and take a risk, but it was a risk I was taking to make my family better, but in a different way. What could be more important than that? I could be the father my daughter needed, and the best husband could be. I wanted to be present for them, building a shared family experience and history. If I squandered this chance, these moments could never be recovered.

I was reminded of "A wise old man that once lived," what the dreamy young version of me wrote for myself as an epitaph. Focusing on these enduring relationships was one path to help move forward to a more complete sense of fulfillment.

Our life plans are so transient. No matter how death comes to us, or other loved ones in our life, that separation is inevitable. Knowing all that, we still struggle to make the most of it. The one common effect of separation, regardless of the reason, is pain for both parties. Our love for them and our time with them are the only impressions that help endure the suffering of inevitable absence. We are all running from one thing to the next, but we are all still in a race against our lack of time here. What would I give to spend time with my mother, father, and niece one more time? What would my wife not give to spend more time with her mother? Is there anything more lasting I can give those I love than my *time*?

Once I realized that, I knew I needed a change. I was a resourceful and effective leader, generally very good at my job, and I knew I would only get better and better; I loved the lifestyle it offered. However, I realized clearly my job was not good for me any longer. My mind, my heart, my body, my soul, everything was crying for intervention. Not letting my life be a run-away train was the right thing to do. Slowing down to be there for my daughter, my wife, my family, my friends was what I wanted.

My happiness and joy come from my sense of purpose arising from these relationships; I truly find myself coming alive in those shared moments. I was unwilling to allow the pain of separation be the price for success any longer. If life is a series of choices, with chance playing some role, then it seems an amalgamation of intent, action, and chance equals life. So, I choose, if these two people are the best things in my life, they are going to come first from then on, no matter what.

It felt this could restore the balance that eluded us until then, and such balance would help lead to sustained happiness. Meena wholeheartedly supported my desire for greater balance. I'd just blown a huge sum of money on a fancy, and now sort of useless, Harvard course only to find out that I needed to find something else to do with my life. In that regard it was the best money we ever spent.

Until then, it felt like I was raised with a purpose, to do something big, and there were so many expectations placed on me. To make this conscious choice at leading a balanced life, was a move I never imagined I would make. Getting to the point of picking a new path professionally for myself while maintaining a rewarding family life was not as easy as it seemed to be.

Having worked as the president of a company for several years by then, and with this Harvard credential, I positioned myself professionally at the final base camp of a great mountain, on my ascent to the highest peaks of my career. While even starting to think along those lines about significant life changes, to walk away from all that was a nerve-wracking first step. Doing it required me to seek the emotional wherewithal to let go financially, earning significantly less.

Doing less prestigious and challenging work was not appealing; I had to work towards overcoming that part of myself. Accepting the loss of identity and self-worth after disassociating from an ego-boosting job, the big title, a big organization to lead isn't quite simple or straightforward. I had to conquer my ego, learn, and believe that it was okay to be average, a happy and content average. Being extra ordinary as a life goal did not make sense any longer. I found myself drawn to a simpler life.

After futile experiments in a different role first and later with different businesses, I decided that property management allowed me to work locally without taking undue financial risks and offered me significantly better control over my time. I dove into the local rental market in Charlotte, some in economic opportunity zones and lower income neighborhoods.

For someone that thrived in a suit and tie professional environment for so many years, it was a major adjustment fitting into the new avatar of "rent guy." This new role allowed me to be part of a social experiment in my own mind, putting me in touch with the less advantaged economic members of the wealthiest nation in the world. I tried my best to be a "good" landlord, choosing to work with tenants that fall behind, showing my compassion towards their difficulties in putting bread on the table, while occasionally weeding out the chronically bad tenants. Without this part of my life there are a whole range of experiences, some funny, some sad, some serious, and some downright dangerous, I would have missed out on.

When it was time to choose my daughter's school, I realized for the first time what my father went through when making these decisions for me years ago. I felt sorry for the situation he was placed in having to make such tough choices for me. Clearly it couldn't have been easy. For my daughter, instead of more prestigious schools in larger cities, we were concerned with parental bonding and love, not simply sending her off to school which would have denied her the very familial bond we were trying to preserve.

Believing that Charlotte will be a good, moderately paced city to raise our child, a place where Meena and I would be able to spend time with her, prioritizing school over waterfront property, we sold our house and moved to *Maitri IV*, across from the school we had decided to send her to. Although my daughter is blessed with a "super mom" who had a limited need for my help with her daily routines, playing the role of my daughter's chauffeur is now one of my favorite pastimes. I also felt vindicated in my choice to focus on a fulfilling family life with my wife and daughter. I was not going to save the best for the last anymore.

I will never be fully comfortable with my choice to not go back to India, for I find my heart still beating for India. But with the sad realization that not much was left for us there following our mother's death, although nothing was explicit, it was clear that none of the family would go back to India. So, eventually my sisters and I decided to sell the family's farm that was gifted to them as dowry, where both my parents and ancestor's remains were laid to rest, bringing an end to our family's generational relationship with that land. Hoping to do something good with it, instead of selling it on the private market, we sold it to the government, so the land could be used to build housing for the poor in the village. I am sure my father and mother would have approved whole heartedly.

In a small attempt to root ourselves in the land of our future, Meena and I bought property with the intent of developing an urban farm near Charlotte. Although, we would never be able to replicate the heritage that went back generations, it felt that connecting back to the land would help establish the same sense of connection we had in India. Given our lack of farming knowledge, the idea was to partner with a local farmer to create a living and working farm that could preserve urban green spaces and promote sustainability and create access to fresh food.

Many people take pride in being "self-made" and I applaud such efforts, mine included. But I never really saw myself as completely self-made. I am the product of my environment, supported by many people including my parents, uncles and aunts, friends, employers, and family that shaped me and believed in me and supported me. Upon hearing my story, a dear friend once said, "It's a mild miracle you ended up the way you did. It was just as likely that you could have ended up a rebel without a cause, or a recluse, or an alcoholic, or a drug addict."

But here I am. Perhaps family was my addiction, and that ended up being a good thing for me, saving me, protecting me, and guiding me during my most vulnerable times. I now see that my family and friends were a source of inspiration, and I tried my best—most of the time, anyway—to not make an idiot of myself.

My father's death during my early childhood made me into a responsible person, an excellent planner and good in a crisis. The chaotic environment at Krishna uncle's house gave me the ability to focus and think things through, the pain of separation from family taught me the value of persistence. Given all the premature deaths we endured, I was engulfed with a fear of people just disappearing, especially after my mother's death.

The fear of catastrophe has only increased after my daughter's birth, I live with a constant fear the next bad thing is always waiting around the corner, ready to attack. I had to learn, unlearn, and relearn many habits and behaviors to overcome the traumas of my childhood insecurities and fears. Death and loss have achieved such an existential status in our lives that I have contemplated the stark realities of death thousands of times, so I am no longer fearful of my own death. I am fearful for Meena and my daughter; my love for them wants me to be there for them as long as I can.

At times, I admit, I feel like I am maybe missing out on something else, more desirable, high powered corporate environment, where I could make a reputation for myself. I might very well regret, at some point, not living up to my full potential and seeking professional success and stardom. I do question if I am on the right path, if I am becoming gradually irrelevant, professionally speaking, having made this choice to focus more on my family and less on the career. Sometimes there is external pressure from Meena concerned that at the end of the day I may end up a dissatisfied soul after all.

I must consciously remind myself as to what I would lose, what I would be sacrificing, what it would all lead to if I pursued a more aggressive path seeking personal glory. Overall, I must say, I am content with the course I chose for myself. Learning to take personal time for myself and my family, giving a higher priority to the quality of my overall life instead of greater glory in a narrower segment of life. And I don't say any of this viewing my life through some rose-colored lenses or as though I am enlightened by some new age life guru. I do realize that of course, my view of my current life is only possible due to my earlier deliberate years of relative frugality. That financial mindset allowed me to gain some independence and develop the ability to cherish the personal time. Without that my mind would have been racing, my thoughts elsewhere, mentally absent, only physically present, always worrying.

This life choice will require a lot of internal struggle. Probably more than is easy to confront, but the source of all restless ego, one's sense of self, is in ones' own mind. It's fueled by how a person desires the world to see them, and how they can propel themselves, while unchecked ego can lead to peril by the deep voids that would be left from not knowing who a person really is and what they really desire.

There are benefits to leading a life with a calmer, quieter mind, focused on the journey rather than the destination but knowing where one wants to end up, without losing sight of the purpose. This wisdom has made my life better, and it has made me a better person as well, a better father, a better husband, a better friend, and a more compassionate version of myself, which I hope to improve on every remaining day of my life.

As much as I would like to claim, I did this selflessly for my daughter, really, I did this for myself. I did it for my health and my sanity and needing to fill a deeper, greater emotion I needed since my childhood. It is possible that should my life demand a rebalance in the future, driving me back towards prioritizing our financial stability over the emotional security I seek, I may pursue that tradeoff once again. As of now, I am still living my life by choice, with the ability and willingness to appreciate and savor the poetry of life, choosing to live, and learning to enjoy things as they are, without throwing up my hands saying there's nothing I can do to make a difference. Most importantly I cherish and respect the small, shared world I have with my family. Doing my utmost to be in the moment, in the present, without obsessing about me and my past or preparing to fight all the monsters my anxieties can conjure up when the future is uncertain.

I would love to imagine my daughter's life will be like walking one long beautiful path strewn with rose petals, or that any of our lives could be, but that's not possible. Her life, like so many, will be filled with elation and tragedy, individual to her but still connected to the people and world around her. I know Meena and I will have done our best to teach her the life skills and personal wherewithal to persevere through individual effort, seeking help when needed, like families have done for generations. I know from painful experience my daughter and wife will be better off with me than without me. We also have the courage to face the world together as a family, no matter what.

Life is a story with many endings, each finale marking the beginning of something new. In my case my daughter has given me new aspirations for future memories and goals, and pushed me to balance my life, true to her name and our belief that everyone lost is born again, we have our dearest Renée.

*The wise observe action in their inaction*
*And inaction in their action*
*Every act is done with*
*Unified consciousness*
*And complete awareness.*

*— The Gita*

# Afterword

LOOKING BACK AT MY PAST traumas and triumphs, I realize it has taken most of my emotional and mental effort to live a life where I had some choices (agency) with a semblance of balance (sanity). Things are simply overwhelming a great deal of the time and there is still more for me to do to process the fear, anxiety, pain, loss, and hope that are the products, intended or not, of simply being alive. Like everyone else I have had to face and overcome the terrifyingly common problems and pain of existence, but in the face of all the difficulties people persevere. In a very real way, the world is made up of ordinary folks heroically defying the odds every day. Luckily, I did too, with, of course, some assistance. No one really ever does anything alone, good, or bad. When all is said and done, I believe that in the end all we have in life are our choices and those we surround ourselves with.

As a young child I was plucked out of my home, taken away from my mother, grandmother, and two younger sisters, by my father who, with the best intentions, but in pursuit of his own dreams for me, sent me away for school to a city hundreds of miles away. This early isolation from my mother and family is an emotional touchstone and, I realized later, significant to how I have made choices in my life. All the subsequent decisions I made pursuing my own dreams put me along a path that necessitated being uprooted and heading to the U.S.

I always seemed to be leaving behind a closely knit family, with whom I had a complex emotional dynamic, but was nevertheless the only one I knew. I had missed out on some significant personal relationships, while achieving incremental material success, and perhaps not surprisingly losing in some ways and gaining in others. It still leaves me wondering if it was all worthwhile.

Having grown up in India, I am from a culture where ancient stories of tragedy and success still hold a great deal of sway. It was impossible not to continually encounter the philosophical notion that one's life is determined by fate or destiny and that things are outside our power to influence what happens in life, whether big or small. Traditional Indian concepts of morality with a long-established reverence and responsibility for one's family favored sons over daughters and even guided decisions related to their children's marriage partners. The cultural acceptance of patriarchy, social hierarchy, and self-worth as well as notions of birth and death run deep.

The role of Karma is still deeply ingrained in many aspects of everyday behavior and belief, even if their origins may be slightly obscured. I felt this even at a young age. I have spent a great deal of time attempting to reconcile those traditions with the modern world, as well with my own decisions about how to live my life. And I definitely had a mind of my own; when I was ten years old, I told my mother I would not be set up in an arranged marriage, which she reluctantly accepted.

I think a sense of independence and dissatisfaction with the traditional view of the world I was presented with, would seem to go together in my case. I all too often wondered, "If everything is preordained, why really bother doing anything?" Instead, I chose to believe that anything worthwhile or meaningful requires individual effort, mental and physical.

Simultaneously, people can only be at their best with a strong network of family and friends, and as I learned from my uncle Indra Babai[12]* who told me, "Don't be bashful in life, it's important to boldly seek help when needed." It's also smart to know when to seek council or support. I was aided by so many people along the way: family, friends, schools, employers, even strangers, without them I would not have made it through. I also came to the firm conclusion that everyone must be given the freedom and guidance to pursue their own way and seek their own balance, each one unique to their individual life experience.

With these things in mind, I have attempted to lead my life in a conscious and deliberate fashion, actively pursuing change every step of the way, with a firm belief that my future was not written. But, not to get too cosmic, I have had to admit there seems to be also the random, unfathomable, and irrational nature of chance or "luck," both good and bad or the physics of time that create a seemingly inescapable and irrevocable finality.

Leaving India taught me that U.S. culture uniquely supports the idea of individual action as a way toward success in pursuit of one's own happiness. At the same time, I had to learn that "success" goes far beyond one's career or material acquisitions. True success is striking a balance between all the competing demands of life and maintaining a state of mind that leaves one open to the possibility of peace and happiness.

In the middle of my path through life, without knowing it, I was on the edge of a precipice, and with little control over what was happening, a horrible loss would once again leave me in crisis at a pivotal juncture. I drifted into feeling purposeless and empty inside. Such moments can define our entire existence, and we all face them in one way or another.

I learned that life is a series of choices, and often ones we would rather not have to make. There are many different paths people take through life. Some boldly take the less traveled ones, and others the more familiar "reliable" ones, everyone fearing the unknown. Sometimes

---

[12] *Babai*, means uncle in Telugu

it seems that regardless of the path taken, or the choices made, they all end in a similar place. It always lurks in the back of my mind whether there is some invisible hand at work that leads to favorable outcomes for some and disastrous ones for others.

When faced with the reality of untimely loss and unexpected death I realized something else deep inside me died as well. I had to find a way to be a person that I could live with. And to acknowledge, after everything I had been through, the reality of how loss and hope shape ourselves and our lives in ways we can't always see, but probably try to. The dualities in my life have molded who I was, who I am, and who I will be.

I, like many Indian immigrants, am the product of two very different worlds. One is the thousands of years' old India's Vedic culture and Bronze age outlook and values, and the other is contemporary global culture with all its advantages and pitfalls. For modern day Indians there is an almost irreconcilable tension between these two worlds. From pursuing the modern "Indian Dream" to having to arrange marriages for my younger sisters, but choosing my own wife, the differences and demands of these two worlds have stayed with me my whole life.

It feels like while juggling the usual unceasing demands of life, one still must cope with the extra stuff the universe seems to throw at us. My story has been played out by literally millions of people, with slight differences, all over the world. In telling my story I hope to: inspire those struggling with similar challenges, give a little insight into the Indian way of life, the history and culture of more than a billion people on this planet, and maybe provide comfort to those suffering loss.

Like many, throughout life I have faced external and internal obstacles. My own fears about failure, loss, separation and making choices have been constant companions. The reality paradoxically was, that for me, achieving the classic immigrant's success story brought about one of my greatest personal crises about who I was. I'm not superhuman and claim no special ability to persevere, rather, much like the rest of the planet I managed to find ways to cope and go forward and most importantly have had close and rewarding family relationships.

When my daughter was born, I realized I had to shift my whole frame of reference to make sense out of anything I was doing. After significant emotional and physical effort, I learned the need to balance all the different demands our lives make on us, especially at important moments. Trying to see all the different pieces involved and still maintain a grasp on the underlying situation is necessary to sustain purpose and meaning. Without maintaining some balance, the clarity of goals can eventually be obscured, and our happiness or satisfaction short lived.

I think the best description of what I learned thus far from experiences both personal and public, is that I see life as perhaps summarized into a deceptively simple equation: Intent + Action + Chance = Life. I imagine as a businessman I like to think of things as being quantifiable and predictable. But like everyone who is trying to cope, we know that life doesn't go our way because we want it to or work for it and that is a difficult but necessary lesson.

The first impulse to write this book, is to tell my daughter, in my own words, something about her family's roots; who she is, why we wanted a child, her ancestors in India and why we came to the U.S. She will never get to meet her grandparents. This is one way for her to get to know them a little, albeit through my lens. I want her to hear how I navigated all the things that came from the lives I wanted her to know about, wonderful and complex as they are, and the motivations behind my choices.

As I attempted to write my story, I realized how easy it was to get somewhat bogged down in the details of some event and how hard that was to read. I initially wrote the story leaving out certain critical personal details and defining moments. Then, I tried again, as fiction, but as was pointed out to me, "Why make stuff up, when you left perfectly good material on the table last time?" That is when I realized my story is intertwined with that of others and the only way can I paint a complete and full picture of my life is to tell part of their stories as well.

Just like everyone else, I too have long periods of emotional darkness and haunting memories that I can't fully reconstruct. But certain events and episodes are vividly front and center in my mind as though they just happened yesterday. So, I chose the "Highlights and Insights" version of the memoir for my own story. There are some details and whole periods of time missing, but one can't include everything. I tried to identify the more important events and emotions, even if they appeared small, I think I got it, but ...

I'm not a famous person or the richest person nor have I sought that. Like everyone, I have had to face life's challenges and get by and try to prosper and be happy. I have been a lifelong student, and whatever I learned, I want to share. My story and my family's struggles and victories gives voice to and resonates with many, many people around the world.

This is not a spiritual book, per se, it's not a tell-all, nor a rags to riches, nor an overly heroic effort overcoming truly impossible obstacles sort of thing (just of course those we all face). There is no villain in this story. Life itself is the villain, in a manner of speaking. It was not overtly, I don't think anyway, written as a therapeutic moment of catharsis, although that can never be completely disregarded with something like this.

I thought it would be difficult at first, but once I started, the words spilled out and memories came back, all I had to do was put pen to paper and write and write. As I said, this was initially for my daughter and to help give her a sense of identity and connectedness (the latter I lacked), and maybe even guidance (writes the hopelessly naive parent). I had so many questions for my father that I never got to ask, I wanted my daughter to hear it from me: my thoughts, my hopes, my desires, my motivations.

*A Father's Cry For Meaning*, is my real-life story of a life by choice; a memoir of love, struggle, chance, determination, and joy as well as grief, lived through a young boy; a father's dream; a mother's resolve; a couple's odyssey and individual perseverance framed by Indian heritage and the immigrant experience. This is the story of many people and my own at the same time, it is everyone's story in one way or another, each one distinct yet connected to the larger, beautiful, and sometimes wonderfully inexplicable world we all inhabit.

# Acknowledgments

TO EACH OF MY FAMILY that's a part of this book, I am grateful for their company, their love, and the invaluable lessons and memories from our journey together. It's only our time that counts and I deeply cherish all our shared moments. To those that we lost over the years, their spirit lives on, their characters coming to life in this beautiful space you are about to enter.

Being a first-time author, I was earnestly keen on as much feedback as possible. With my characteristically impatient rush, I chose to crowdsource early by recruiting an army of beta readers to pilot test the half-baked draft versions of the manuscript at multiple stages. Anyone within my network who graciously volunteered their time to review the text was welcomed with open arms, believing such enthusiastic reader opinion was critical to improving the narration and the content. I am hugely indebted to everyone that supported me in this painful process with their diligent efforts.

To begin with, I must thank my dear daughter for repeatedly reminding me to make my book funny, like the many silly stories I tell her, and that my memoir should be hilarious like Trevor Noah's and then everyone would love it. I am positive she will be disappointed at dad's inability in fulfilling this one wish of hers. My sincere regards to all my friends who took the time to understand every facet of the story to the intended depth and gave me valuable suggestions, enthusiastically entertaining my relentless queries, particularly, Mike, Mark, Sheridan, Vasanta, Ward, Yvonne, Chandra, Tara, Ellen, Sahiti, Anne, Madhu, Lauren, Karen, Satish, Durga, and Anita.

# About the Author

Sri Burugapalli is a relentless seeker and teacher, a lifelong student of philosophy and human psychology.

Sri is a distinguished business leader in a wide range of industries backed by top tier academic foundation including an MBA from Duke University and an AMP from Harvard Business School. Sri has deep expertise in entrepreneurial startup environments and legacy enterprise turnarounds and is known for his corporate leadership, strategic thinking, financial acumen, client & employee relationships.

Sri spends his best time with his daughter, wife, and family dog; he also writes poetry.

*A Father's Cry for Meaning* is Sri Burugapalli's first book.

# You Might Also Enjoy

### RICE PAPER WINDOW

Christabel Choi

*Christabel Choi enters South Korea as a student in 1989 with a copy of the Communist Manifesto among the books in her bag. She doesn't realize that it could get her—or anyone she might lend it to—arrested or disappeared.*

### BACK TO THE LAND IN SILICON VALLEY

Marlene Anne Bumgarner

*Follow Marlene and her friends as they live on the land, coping with the challenges of rural life as Silicon Valley evolves into the high-tech center it is today.*

### DAILY FRESH

Jory Post

*In the summer of 2020, the final summer of his life, Jory Post gave himself an assignment: He would write one essay a day, inspired by whatever caught his eye and imagination.*

Available from Paper Angel Press in
hardcover, trade paperback, and digital editions
paperangelpress.com